D1022249

Presented to:

....

From:

....

Date:

....

ANNE GRAHAM LOTZ

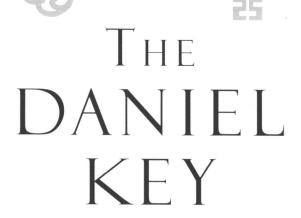

THE
DANIEL
KEY

20 CHOICES THAT
MAKE ALL THE DIFFERENCE

ZONDERVAN®
.com

The Daniel Key
Copyright © 2018 by Anne Graham Lotz

Requests for information should be addressed to:
Zondervan, 3900 Sparks Dr., SE, Grand Rapids, MI 49546

ISBN 978-0-310-09193-6

Cover and Interior design: Kristy Edwards

Printed in China

18 19 20 21 22 / AMY / 20 19 18 17 16 15 14 13 12 11 10 9 8 7 6 5 4 3 2 1

CONTENTS

FINDING THE KEYS
TO SUCCESS

Every day we make multiple choices, from the time we choose to get out of bed in the morning, to the time we choose to go back to bed in the evening. Some choices are practical, some are emotional, some are social. But the ones that make all the difference in life are our moral and spiritual choices. These choices, in a very real way, determine our character and our success as human beings.

Choices are like a spiritual, moral workout. In a physical workout, to strengthen my upper body, I do a series of repetitions with stiff rubber bands. If I pull the band once or twice, I could say it doesn't make any difference, so why go to the trouble? Just one or two pulls actually don't make any difference. But if I pull on them again and again, in a series of repetitions, day after day, they effectively begin to build muscle mass. The difference can actually become visible as I grow stronger.

Like pulling on those bands, our choices are

effective when made again and again, day after day. The repetition of right choices builds our character and strengthens our faith. The repetition of wrong choices can weaken and destroy us. Increasingly, others will be able to see the difference our choices are making.

Daniel was a man who made right choices again and again. Many of us grew up knowing Daniel as the courageous man whose steadfast belief in the one true God got him thrown into a lions' den—and also saved him from those hungry lions. But Daniel's miraculous adventure in the lions' den was just one brief episode in a life that stretched for decades, included several other miracles, and changed history. From Heaven's perspective, there is surely no greater prophet in the Old Testament than Daniel.

Daniel was taken into captivity with the nation of Judah when he was just a teenager. He lived the rest of his life as a slave in Babylon. As such, Daniel wasn't free to make many choices. But the choice he *could* and *did* make at a very early age was to place his faith in God. That initial choice was followed by many others, some of which were hard, critical, and even death-defying. But the end result was a man

whose character and faith were so strong that he stands out as a colossal giant in history.

In this little book, I share twenty of the key choices I found as I studied the life of Daniel when I wrote *The Daniel Prayer*—choices that were keys to his success. They are choices that not only work today, but that will also make all the difference in whether you and I are sterling in character, strong in our faith, and successful in life—from Heaven's perspective.

CHAPTER 1

Faith MAKES A DIFFERENCE

And without faith it is impossible to please God, because anyone who comes to him must believe that he exists and that he rewards those who earnestly seek him.

HEBREWS 11:6

F aith is not a "gift" that some people have been given and others have not. Faith is a choice that becomes a lifestyle of trusting God.

This wonderful truth reminds me of a favorite story. It's about the French tightrope walker Charles Blondin, the first person to cross Niagara Falls on a tightrope. The cable stretched 1,300 feet across and far above the raging waters straddling the border between the United States and Canada. When he made it across, crowds on both the American and the Canadian sides roared at his success.

Blondin walked across the falls several more times on subsequent dates. On one of those dates, he prepared to push a wheelbarrow across the rope. The crowd's cheers grew louder and more enthusiastic as he asked his roaring fans, "Do you think I could carry a person across in this wheelbarrow?"

"Absolutely!" was the confident response.

"Okay," said Blondin. "Who wants to get in?"

At that question, the crowd was quiet. No one volunteered.

Everyone in the crowd had said they had faith that

Blondin could carry a man over the falls in his wheelbarrow, but that so-called faith evaporated when they were asked to sit in the wheelbarrow.

Real faith is more than just words—or rituals or going to church or having a religion or believing there is a God. Real faith gets in the wheelbarrow: real faith backs up a confident declaration with actions, or it's not real faith (James 2:20). Like exercising a spiritual muscle, real faith grows as we make choice after choice after choice. Those choices can make all the difference.

I made my first real choice of faith when I was eight or nine years old. After watching a film about the life of Christ, I chose to confess to God in prayer that I knew I was a sinner, that I was sorry, and that I was claiming the death of Jesus Christ on the Cross as His sacrifice for my sin. I asked Him to forgive me, then I invited Jesus to come into my heart and life.

This choice led to a second choice to read my Bible daily. Besides strengthening my small seedling of faith, this practice began my lifelong love affair with the Scriptures.

That choice led to another choice I made when I was about fifteen. I was with a group

of friends listening to a guest speaker at the church where I was raised.

We were attending a youth meeting on a Saturday morning, and the speaker was a distinguished professor of divinity at Yale University. All of us were interested in hearing what he had to say.

I can't remember what began to alarm me, but I do remember my heart pounding out of my chest when he said that there was a god for the Old Testament, another god for the New Testament, and a different god for today.

> Like a spiritual muscle, faith grows strong through the exercise of choice after choice after choice.

Without thinking, I jumped to my feet and, interrupting him, said that was not what the Bible taught. In an extremely condescending voice modulated to intimidate me, he inquired, "And just what do you think the Bible says?"

God quickly brought to my mind the words of a verse I had read, and I answered: "The Bible says that Jesus Christ is the same yesterday, today, and forever" (Hebrews 13:8).

The speaker had a startled, somewhat offended yet

quizzical look on his face, as if to say, "Who has dared to challenge me?" That's when my friends pulled on my shirt. "Anne!" they whispered. "Sit down! He's a professor from Yale, for goodness' sake. Be quiet!" So I sat down. I may have been silent on the outside, but I was still arguing on the inside.

About two years after I had confronted the Yale professor, I made a life-defining choice of faith when I knelt down by the window seat in my bedroom and surrendered my life for service to Jesus Christ, a decision that I continue to live out on a daily basis. Thus began a lifetime of choices, some small, some large, some public, some private, but each one seemed to build on the last one, growing and strengthening my faith until . . .

I was able to step onto the platform of an international congress, face ten thousand evangelists while the who's who of the evangelical world sat behind me, and confidently proclaim the words God had given me.

I was able to place my unresponsive husband on an EMS gurney, command the responders to stand still for a moment while I prayed, then allow them to put him in the ambulance, confident that his life was in God's hands and that God would take care of him.

I was able to confront the president of the United States publicly when he misquoted the Scripture as saying that the beginning of wisdom is toleration of others. I felt as if I were fifteen years old all over again, yet this time, in the East Room of the White House, there were no friends to pull me down. The religious leaders who filled the room were so silent you could hear a pin drop, as I took four minutes to explain that the Bible says the beginning of wisdom is the fear of God (Psalms 111:10; Proverbs 1:7, 9:10).

I was able to stand at the podium of the United Nations General Assembly and present the Gospel as the only way to have genuine, permanent world peace—and then to finish my prepared three-minute remarks even after my mic was turned off.

I could not have confronted the president nor addressed the United Nations gathering when I was fifteen years old—or even fifteen years before I had those opportunities. I know God has enabled some Christians to grow up in their faith very quickly, but He has graciously allowed my faith to develop over a lifetime of choices.

While you may not have the luxury of a lifetime

ahead of you to make the critical choices that will develop your faith, it's important that you start now. One choice at a time. God knows how long you will have to develop your faith, and He will make sure that it's sufficient. But you must start now.

THINK ABOUT IT

If you rarely exercise your faith through the choices you make, how can you be surprised when it's too weak to please God? Too weak to face a crisis triumphantly? Too weak to move others to recognize and acknowledge that your God is *the* God? Too weak to be contagious? Daniel's repeated choice to place his faith in God, regardless of how difficult or dangerous the situation was, impresses me that he wanted to serve a God who is God. If God was unable to come through for him—if He was unable to "push the wheelbarrow across the tightrope over Niagara Falls"—then He wasn't a God worth knowing. Or serving. Or risking his life for.

God of Daniel,

I worship you as the foundation of all real faith.

Thank You for making Yourself accessible to all of us through a simple choice: the choice to take You at Your Word, trusting You completely to be who You say You are. Thank You for encouraging my faith by the stories of others who chose to place their faith in You and found You to be utterly trustworthy.

I choose now to climb into the wheelbarrow. I choose to place my faith in You.

Please help my choices from this moment on to so strengthen my faith that my life would be an example that encourages others to choose to place their faith in You, too. Make my faith contagious.

For the glory of Your great name, Amen.

CHAPTER 2

Worship MAKES A DIFFERENCE

Yet a time is coming and has now come when the true worshipers will worship the Father in spirit and truth, for they are the kind of worshipers the Father seeks.

JOHN 4:23

Having been raised in the Blue Ridge Mountains of western North Carolina, I have always loved to hike. When I was young, every Sunday afternoon my entire family, including one or more dogs, would hike to the ridge behind our home. I loved the woodsy smell of the leaves as I scuffed my shoes through them. I loved the roaring sound that grew louder the closer we got to the ridge, where there was no barrier to break the fierce intensity of the wind. I loved looking for box turtles half-submerged in the muddy runoff of the springs beside the old logging road.

When we made it to the end of the road, we hiked the last several hundred feet on a trail where the trees were thick and we had to walk single file. To make sure I was going in the right direction, I had to keep my eyes on Daddy, who always went first. I knew if I kept my eyes centered on him, eventually I would come out at the bare place on top of the mountain that Mother had named the Reed Field, where we could see all the way down the Swannanoa Valley to Asheville. I learned early in life that it's necessary to have a center point when hiking in thick woods. Daddy was my center point.

This lesson was confirmed when I was a teenager. I was on a fourteen-mile hike with a friend. We started behind my parents' home, climbed to the top of the mountain known as Little Piney Ridge, then hiked the ridgelines of the Seven Sisters to Graybeard. The path my friend had chosen was not marked, so we just kept to the highest points along the mountain range. We knew eventually we would come to the trail that led up to Graybeard, the top of which on a clear day has a spectacular view of multiple states.

About an hour before we reached our destination, we got lost in a laurel thicket. While that may sound humorous, it wasn't. Laurel bushes are low and thick, and they can cover the side of a mountain. It's impossible to see out of them in any direction. So my friend pulled out a compass. She adjusted it so that the needle pointed north, then motioned for me to follow her. As she kept her eye on the compass, we fought our way through the bushes. North was our center point. As long as we kept the needle on the compass pointed in that direction, we were able to hike to a place where we could get a better perspective of where we were and subsequently found the trail

we were looking for. Eventually we made it successfully to the top of Graybeard.

If prayer is life's compass, then the needle that points north is the focus of our faith in prayer on the living God. He is the "north" on our "compass." When our prayers are focused, regardless of what life throws at us, whether it's a long, hard climb to the top of our profession or career, or the steady trail of perseverance as we set out to achieve our goals, or the confusion and lost feeling that can envelop us when we find ourselves in a thicket of problems and pressures and pain—if our prayers are focused on worship of the living God, they will make a difference. In us. In our circumstances. In others. In our church. In our nation. In our world.

> **If the needle of our compass is set to point to ourselves or to our circumstances, we will get lost.**

Years ago, I adopted the habit of beginning virtually every prayer I pray with worship. As I center on the One to whom I'm speaking, I try to think of the specific attributes of His character that would be relevant to my prayer. For instance, if I'm burdened for my

children, I address Him as my heavenly Father, worshipping Him as a parent who is supremely patient, loving, and good yet has children who are not perfect. He understands parental agony and heartbreak. If I'm hurt and wounded, I address Him as the One who was wounded for my transgressions, bruised for my iniquities, who understands the feelings of my pain, and who has promised to heal my broken heart. If I have just been blessed or honored, I address Him as the Fountainhead of all blessings, the Giver of every good thing. If I am coming to Him aware I've sinned, before even confessing it to Him, I worship Him as the God of mercy and grace who loves sinners, who is never surprised by my failure because that's all He expects of me in my flesh, who stands ready to pardon and cleanse all those who come to Him by faith at the foot of the Cross.

It's amazing how the simple exercise of putting my focus on who God is helps put my prayer into perspective. My problems don't seem so overwhelming. My questions don't seem so critical. My worries don't seem so all-consuming. My fears don't seem so paralyzing. Centering on Him brings peace and calmness

to my spirit. In the quietness, very often I hear His whisper as He directs me out of the "laurel thicket."

On the other hand, if you begin your prayer focusing on the doctor's grim prognosis for your loved one, or on the probability of a conflict with your child's teacher, or on the impact of the company's downsizing of your job, or on the seemingly nonstop environmental disasters in our nation, or on the increasing prevalence of active shooters, or on the raw savagery of radical militant jihadists, you will melt down to the point that you have no faith whatsoever that your prayers will make any difference at all. For all of us, the outcome of our focus makes our worries and fears appear to be inevitable. The enemy just seems too powerful. The result? If you are like me, you develop a nauseous knot in the pit of your stomach and get lost emotionally and spiritually in the laurel thicket.

One key reason that Daniel's prayer made a difference was because Daniel's faith was centered on the living God. Before Daniel even gave us the words of his prayer, he made it clear that he first "turned to the Lord God" (9:3). He set his compass. As he prayed, he addressed "the great and awesome God, who keeps his covenant of love with all who love him and obey

his commands"; the One who is "righteous"; "the Lord our God [who] is merciful and forgiving" (9:4, 7, 9). The needle of his compass kept pointing north.

THINK ABOUT IT

When do you set your compass? Do you turn to others before you turn to the Lord God? Set the needle of your compass. Turn to God in worship first. Then keep turning to Him in prayer.

We worship You, great God of creation. You were in the beginning. You will be at the end. You always have been, and You always will be. You are the Creator who brings forth something out of nothing, who formed man from dust, who turns darkness into light, who makes the world turn, who sustains all things by Your powerful word.[1]

We worship You alone. We set the needle of our compass on You . . . and You alone.

In the darkness, You are our Light.
In the storm, You are our Anchor.
In the face of terrorism, You are our Shield.

In time of war, You are our Peace.
In our weakness, You are our Strength.
In our grief, You are our Comfort.
In our despair, You are our Hope.
In our confusion, You are our Wisdom.
In times of uncertainty, when . . .
buildings implode,

bombs explode,
stock markets slide,
people commit suicide,
banks collapse,
businesses are bankrupted,
and homes are foreclosed . . .

*When the nations rage and the people
imagine a vain thing . . .*

*When the rulers take a stand and gather
together against the Lord . . .* [2]

When the earth gives way . . .

*When the mountains fall into the midst of
the sea . . .*

When the waters roar and foam . . .

*When nations are in uproar and kingdoms
fall . . .* [3]

When everything gives way,
You are the Rock on which we stand!

*Help us keep the needle of our faith
pointed to You.*

For the glory of Your great name,
Amen.

CHAPTER 3

Loyalty MAKES A DIFFERENCE

LORD, the God of our fathers Abraham, Isaac and Israel, keep this desire in the hearts of your people forever, and keep their hearts loyal to you.

1 CHRONICLES 29:18

When Daniel was approximately fifteen years old, a history-changing event radically altered his life in ways he would never have imagined.

Babylonian troops had surrounded Jerusalem and conquered it. They'd then gathered the city's most intelligent, gifted, personable, handsome, capable young men and transported them back to Babylon to serve in King Nebuchadnezzar's court. Daniel and three of his friends—Shadrach, Meshach, and Abednego—were caught up in what is known as the *first deportation* when enemy soldiers led approximately two hundred young Jewish men from Jerusalem to Babylon, where they were enslaved.

When Daniel arrived in the capital city of his nation's enemy, he was immediately plunged into an intense three-year brainwashing program. In an effort to cut him off from his past and assimilate him into the Babylonian culture, Daniel was stripped of his Hebrew name, which meant "God is my judge," and renamed Belteshazzar, a cry to the wife of the Babylonian god Bel. It was an unveiled effort to weaken, if not destroy, Daniel's faith in his God.

At the same time, Daniel was probably stripped of his masculinity. The fact that his immediate supervisor was the "master of [the] eunuchs" implies that Daniel himself was one (Daniel 1:3 NKJV). This heartless act was surely intended to humiliate Daniel and force him into a subservient position that communicated clearly that his only purpose in life was to serve Nebuchadnezzar. Daniel would not be distracted by a wife or children.

While it was impossible for Daniel to prevent either the changing of his name or his emasculation, he could and did take a stand regarding his diet:

God honors those who honor Him.

he would not eat the king's food that had first been sacrificed to idols. Eating food offered to idols was an indirect way of paying them tribute. Because Daniel's faith was centered in the living God of Abraham, Isaac, and Jacob, to give tribute to other gods, even indirectly, would be to betray and deny his own God. So Daniel "resolved not to defile himself with the royal food and wine, and he asked the chief official for permission not to defile himself this way" (1:8).

Daniel's faith was more than just lip-service,

more than just rituals or tradition. And so, Daniel requested a different diet. As reasonable and harmless as that sounds, Daniel made his request at the risk of his very life. Ashpenaz, the chief eunuch, explained to Daniel that the king himself had assigned the food and that to reject it for a substitute diet "would endanger my head with the king" (1:10 ESV).

At that point Daniel could easily have told God, "Well, I tried. You know in my heart I'm not paying tribute to these false gods, but I have to eat to survive." He could have simply eaten the king's food. Certainly it may have tasted better! But he refused. His choice was to reject the compromise of his faith (the king's food)—to reject the betrayal of his God. It was born out of his choice to be loyal to his God regardless of wherever he was or whatever he was confronted with and whoever disagreed or threatened him.

Daniel did not back down. After Ashpenaz denied his request, Daniel went to his guard and suggested an experiment. He asked the guard to serve him and his three friends a simple diet of vegetables and water. If, after ten days, he and his friends were not better off than the other young captives who ate the king's food, the guard could do whatever he chose.

God honored Daniel's loyalty and prompted the guard to agree. Ten days later when they were evaluated, Daniel, Shadrach, Meshach, and Abednego "looked healthier and better nourished than any of the young men who ate the royal food" (1:15). The four remained on that diet, and three years later, when the king himself gave them their final exams "in every matter of wisdom and understanding . . . , he found them ten times better than all the magicians and enchanters that were in all his kingdom" (1:20 ESV). Loyalty to God made all the difference.

THINK ABOUT IT

When faced with loyalty to God that puts you in conflict with those who are in authority over you, what is your choice?

God of Glory,

I worship You as a living person. You are all-powerful and all-knowing. You are glorious. Majestic. Holy. You are seated on the throne of Heaven. The entire universe reverberates with praise of You. One day it will be my highest privilege and deepest joy to join in the throng of millions upon millions of people who bow before Your throne and to lift my voice in adoration of the One who alone is worthy of all praise and honor and glory and power and wisdom and wealth!

Thank You for the promise that on That Day, if I have acknowledged You before others, You will acknowledge me before the universe.[1]

Thank You for inviting me even now to enter into Your presence through prayer.

I ask that You give me a stronger conscious awareness of who You are than of who I am. Help me to care more about what You think and say than about the opinions of others.

I choose to be loyal to You at any cost, knowing that on That Day whatever price I have paid will be worth it!

For the glory of Your great name, Amen.

CHAPTER 4

Prayer Partners
MAKE A
DIFFERENCE

"For where two or three come together in my name, there am I with them."

MATTHEW 18:20

Daniel and his three friends had established a prayer partnership. We are given a glimpse of this partnership when King Nebuchadnezzar had a dream that was deeply disturbing to him.

When the king awoke from his bad dream, he called in all of his counselors, demanding that they tell him his dream and what it meant. His astounded counselors declared they could possibly give him the interpretation of the dream but he would first need to tell them what the dream was. But the enraged king was adamant that the wise men should be able to both discern what his dream had been and tell him what it meant. Even when he threatened to cut them into pieces and turn their houses into piles of rubble if they did not do what he demanded, the terrified astrologers knew they could not do what the king required. Death was staring them in the face. Surely with horror in their eyes, with knees turned to jelly, with hearts that melted within their chests and heads that spun dizzily, they must have gasped as they gave their emphatic answer: "There is not a man on earth who can do what the king

asks!" (2:10). Furiously, the king ordered the execution of all the wise men in Babylon. And because that was Daniel's category of service, it meant that he and his three friends had just been given a death sentence.

Under orders from the king, the military commander came to arrest Daniel and carry out the execution. Daniel did not run. He did not try to escape. He did not organize a band of rebels and revolt against such irrational injustice. Instead, Daniel respectfully inquired why. When the commander explained, Daniel requested an audience with the king, asking for time to consider the matter. The king's lingering fear over what his dream could mean must have overruled his rage, and he agreed. While everyone's life hung in the balance, Daniel asked his three friends to pray. They did pray, and it made all the difference.

> To achieve a breakthrough, sometimes we need reinforcements.

By morning light, God had given the dream and its interpretation to Daniel. His emotional relief punctuated his morning prayer in heartfelt, overflowing thanksgiving:

Praise be to the name of God for ever and ever;
wisdom and power are his. He changes times and
seasons; he sets up kings and deposes them. He gives
wisdom to the wise and knowledge to the discern-
ing. He reveals deep and hidden things, he knows
what lies in darkness, and light dwells with him.
I thank and praise you, O God of my fathers: You
have given me wisdom and power, you have made
known to me what we asked of you, you have made
known to us the dream of the king (2:20–23).

When Daniel went to the king, Nebuchadnezzar's
eyes must have narrowed as he looked very skeptically
at this young Israelite slave and asked him, "Are you
able to tell me what I saw in my dream and interpret
it?" (2:26). Daniel's fearless answer reveals his rock-
solid confidence in God when he replied, "No wise
man, enchanter, magician or diviner can explain to
the king the mystery he has asked about, but there is
a God in heaven who reveals mysteries. He has shown
King Nebuchadnezzar what will happen in days to
come" (2:27–28). Then Daniel proceeded to describe
the dream and its meaning.

The result? The king was astounded! He confirmed

Daniel had accurately described his dream; therefore, the interpretation must also be accurate. And it was. More significantly, God was glorified as the king acknowledged that Daniel's God is the God of gods and the King of kings. And Daniel was honored by being made ruler over all of Babylon.

The prayers of Daniel's three friends combined with his own made all the difference.

THINK ABOUT IT

Do you have a prayer partner, someone you can call to pray with you either on a regular basis or in an emergency? If not, ask God to bring to your mind someone who can pray for you, and for whom you can pray. A prayer partnership can make all the difference.

Great High Priest,

We worship You as our Mediator,[1] the One who ever lives to make intercession for us.[2] You are our invisible Prayer Partner. What would or could we ever do without You?

You know our weakness. And You know the enemy's strength. You know that in ourselves we can't seem to achieve the breakthrough that we desperately desire. Your answers seem elusive. as though there is a blockage in the heavenly realm. We need help.

I remember when You sent out Your disciples, You sent them out two by two, knowing they needed each other in physical, emotional, and spiritual ways as they served You. And You have commanded us to "pray for each other,"[3] knowing that as we engage in spiritual warfare on our knees, we also need the strength, wisdom, insight, discernment, support, and encouragement that are uniquely available when we pray with a partner.

Please, would You now bring to my mind the name of someone whom I could partner with in prayer, someone to whom I could be an encouragement, and who could, in turn, encourage me? Prepare his or her heart to receive my offer, so that our partnership will make a difference as we achieve spiritual breakthrough.

For the glory of Your great name, Amen.

CHAPTER 5

Praying for Others MAKES A DIFFERENCE

I urge, then, first of all, that requests, prayers, intercession and thanksgiving be made for everyone. . . . This is good, and pleases God our Savior.

1 TIMOTHY 2:1, 3

Daniel poured out his heart in prayer for his people. Again and again, he used plural pronouns as he prayed, in the end concluding: "Give ear, O God, and hear. . . . O Lord, listen! O Lord, forgive! . . . For your sake, O my God, do not delay, because your city and your people bear your Name" (9:18–19). As a result, God's people were blessed beyond measure because Daniel had interceded for them.

Intercession has been compared to "plowing up the ground." Any farmer can attest to the importance of plowing the ground before planting crops each spring. For me, it was a lesson I learned best from my grandfather.

We called my grandfather on my father's side Daddy Graham. He was a tall, gentle, soft-spoken, true Southern gentleman. Daddy Graham wore black-and-white spectator shoes and a broad-brimmed hat pulled down on his brow, but only when he was going to church or to the nearby S & W Cafeteria. For most of the week, he dressed in faded, well-worn work clothes that carried with them the "sweet essence of agriculture" because he was a dairy farmer.

I was raised hearing from my father how Daddy Graham had made him get up at three o'clock every morning to milk about fourteen cows before he went to school. Daddy didn't have an alarm to wake him up. What he had was the warning from Daddy Graham that if he overslept he would get a bucket of cold water in his face. Which he did. Once. From then on, Daddy was up on time.

Daddy Graham also grew the corn that he fed to his cows. The hottest I've ever been was when I walked through the cornfield next to my grandparents' house one summer afternoon. I can verify that in the heart of a cornfield, there is no breeze at all. Just stifling heat. When I emerged from the field, I was

> **Effective intercession is offered with wet eyes, a broken heart, and bent knees.**

dripping wet and covered with what felt like tiny paper cuts that the stiff leaves of the cornstalks had left on my arms. That was in the summertime. But after the corn was harvested, the ground in that cornfield was left bare and became hardened. Within a fairly short period of time, weeds and grass would begin to take over. Before Daddy Graham could plant the next crop

of corn the following spring, he had to plow up the fallow earth and remove the weeds until the ground was soft enough to receive the seeds of corn, which he would then plant so they could absorb the rain and sunshine that he hoped would follow.

The nation of Judah had once been like a fertile field that had grown "crops" of righteousness—people who loved, obeyed, and served the Lord. But as a result of Judah's sin, God had raised up the Babylonians as His instruments of judgment. The consequences were that Daniel and his people were removed and taken eight hundred miles east, where they were enslaved in a foreign land. In essence, the land and the people had lain "fallow," unplowed for sixty-seven years.

So Daniel made the choice to intercede for his people . . .

To plow up the fallow ground.

To plead with God to forgive their sin, deliver them from judgment, "heal the land," and bring life back to Jerusalem.

To beg God to return to the center of their national life by reviving authentic worship and restoring the temple.

Bottom line: Daniel's intercession was a plea for God to be glorified once again through the people's personal and national lives. It was a prayer for national restoration and revival.

If that sounds familiar, it's because again and again, over the last few years, we have heard God's promise to King Solomon in 2 Chronicles 7:14 invoked on behalf of our nation: "If my people, who are called by my name, will humble themselves and pray and seek my face and turn from their wicked ways, then I will hear from heaven and will forgive their sin and will heal their land." I have used that promise. I have prayed it. I have claimed it. I have built messages around it. It was a foundational verse for a prayer I wrote that was prayed in more than forty-four thousand services for our nation in 2014.[1]

Yet instead of experiencing revival, why does our nation seem to be collapsing until we are morally and spiritually bankrupt? Why are we witnessing a hell-bent charge into the miry pits of sin and secularism? Why, instead of being healed, have we seemed to become more polarized than ever? I wonder . . . Have we

been missing something? Overlooking . . . neglecting . . . ignoring something?

Out of the sixteen verses covered by Daniel's magnificent prayer of intercession in chapter 9, twelve of them confess sin. Not "their" sin, but "our" sin. All through his prayer, Daniel uses plural pronouns, which reveals to me that he was as aware of sin in his own heart as he was in the hearts of his people. There was nothing judgmental or self-righteous in his words. Instead, Daniel prayed with the words of a man who seemed to have a conscious awareness of his own sin as he prayed for the sin he saw in others. Could that be what's missing in our prayers of intercession? I wonder.

THINK ABOUT IT

We may never have another Great Awakening in our nation until you and I stop pointing our fingers at "them" and deal with the sin in our own hearts and lives. An old-timey revivalist, Gypsy Smith, was asked where revival begins.

He answered, "I draw a circle around myself and make sure everything in that circle is right with God." Which begs the question: if we have yet to see revival fire fall in our nation, could the problem be within the circle?

Great, Eternal High Priest,

Save us from ourselves.
Free us from the chokehold of sin.
Protect us from our enemies.
Spare us from Your judgment.
We are pleading with You for an
outpouring of Your Spirit on us, on
our families, on our churches, and on
our nation. Send down Your Spirit in
Pentecostal fullness! Captivate us by Your
love! Rend our hearts with deep conviction
and sorrow for our sin! Draw us back to
the foot of the Cross. Plunge us beneath the
fountain filled with His blood, then . . .

Revive our hearts!
Fill our hearts!
Ignite our hearts. . .

with a pure and holy passion to love
You and to live our lives for You, and for
Your glory alone!

Then use us to bring revival to the
hearts of Your people!

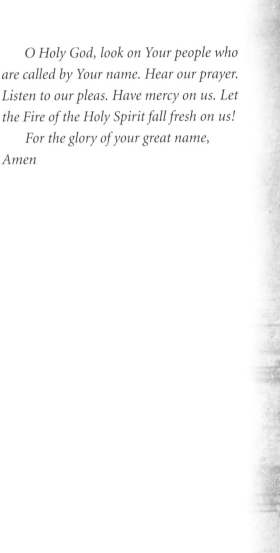

O Holy God, look on Your people who are called by Your name. Hear our prayer. Listen to our pleas. Have mercy on us. Let the Fire of the Holy Spirit fall fresh on us!

For the glory of your great name,
Amen

CHAPTER 6

Praying God's Word MAKES A DIFFERENCE

I, Daniel, understood from the Scriptures, according to the word of the Lᴏʀᴅ given to Jeremiah the prophet, that the desolation of Jerusalem would last seventy years. So I turned to the Lord God and pleaded with him in prayer.

DANIEL 9:2–3

Daniel could not have understood God's word given to Jeremiah if he had not been reading it. One reason I always take my Bible into my prayer time is because I want to listen to what God has to say about whatever is on my heart, and then take what He says and pray it back to Him. For example:

When I struggled with infertility, longing to get pregnant, but month after month did not, God gave me a promise in 1 Samuel 1:17 that He would grant what I had asked of Him. In answer to prayer, He kept His word. In time, I not only gave birth to a son, but to two daughters.

When I was confined to a small home with small children and deeply desired to serve the Lord, He revealed from Hosea 2:14 that He had intentionally placed me in the "wilderness" so that He could speak to me

> **Praying God's Word back to Him is like reversing thunder.**

and I would learn to listen to His voice. His Word was true. I did not waste my wilderness years but studied the

Scriptures, and thus was prepared when He called me out to teach the Bible to others.

When the door of service was opened and I found myself in the pulpit, looking at five hundred upturned, expectant faces waiting to hear what I was going to say, He clearly confirmed my call in Jeremiah 1:4–7 to go wherever He sent me and to say whatever He commanded me. I was not to be afraid of their faces. Although my timidity and shyness caused me to be physically sick before I spoke for the first six weeks of teaching, I remembered His Word and did not give in to the fear.

When I stood on the platform in a soccer field in India, a race track in Australia, a prison auditorium in North Carolina, the General Assembly of the United Nations, the funeral service for my mother, and many, many other places where I was in way over my head, He assured me from John 3:34 that He would give me His Spirit without limit. I have experienced His promised sufficiency for more than forty years as He has always been faithful to equip, enable, and empower me to be fully obedient to His call.

Daniel held God to His word, and three years after his prayer that was based on Jeremiah 29:10–12, God answered. His people were set free to return to Jerusalem.

THINK ABOUT IT

On what are your prayers based? Your hopes? Your dreams? Your wishes? Your wants? Your thoughts? Are they based on what someone else says or thinks or does or wants? Could that be why your prayers are anemic? The next time you pray, open up your Bible. Ask God to give you a promise. Then claim it as you pray it back to Him.

Lord of the Ages . . . Living Word,

We worship You as the One who is Truth. You are the Light. In You is no darkness at all—no spin, no lies, no deception, no falsity.

Thank You for your promises that are ever true. They are more precious than gold.

We ask that You would teach us to pray according to Your Word. We want to ask You for what You have already purposed to give us, to do for us, and to do through us, yet will not do so until we ask. We don't want to get to Heaven and discover all the answers to prayer for which we never bothered to ask You, because we were ignorant of Your Word.[1]

So speak, Lord, as we, Your children, listen with our eyes on the pages of our Bibles . . .

For the glory of Your great name, Amen.

CHAPTER 7

Attitude MAKES A DIFFERENCE

Your attitude should be the same as that of Christ Jesus.

PHILIPPIANS 2:5

Do you need an attitude check? Especially, when . . .

life throws you a curveball? Are you thankful?

your expectations, goals, and dreams have not been realized? Are you thankful?

your life's circumstances go from bad to worse? Are you thankful?

your critics are watching every move you make, eager to catch you in something they can use to discredit you? Are you thankful?

you are enslaved by a body of pain or a demanding employer? Are you thankful?

How could anyone have a positive, thankful attitude under those circumstances?

Remarkably, Daniel did. He made a habit of giving thanks to God three times a day. Think about it. We are given a glimpse of his attitude of gratitude when his enemies were lurking outside his window, plotting his death (6:1–28). He was more than eighty years old and still enslaved eight hundred miles from home. He served a ruthless king who had destroyed his beloved city and butchered countless people, many of whom

I'm sure Daniel had known personally. None of the dreams he had had for himself growing up as a boy in Jerusalem would ever be realized. At the stage in his life when we see him on his knees in prayer, he must have also come to the rude awakening that he would never go home. He would never see Jerusalem again. *Yet he was thankful?* How could that be?

The key to thankfulness is not to view God through the lens of our circumstances, but to view our circumstances through the lens of God's love and sovereign purpose. God had called

> **Our attitude today can determine our greatness . . . or smallness . . . tomorrow.**

Daniel, not to a life of comfort and ease, but to a life of greatness. And so Daniel could thank God for everything in his life. He knew, as he entered his winter years, that all things had worked together for his good in order to enable him to fulfill God's purpose.[1]

As a result, Daniel did indeed live a life of greatness. From Heaven's perspective, there is no greater prophet in the Old Testament than Daniel. We are still referring to his prophecies to make sense of what we see happening in our world today. And he was

great in the eyes of his own world. With God's favor, he rose quickly through the Babylonian system so that he stood out with exceptional distinction among the many other exiles captured from Judah. During his lifetime, he served as a counselor to the king, as a provincial governor in Babylon, then as prime minister under Nebuchadnezzar, Belshazzar (for one night), Darius, and Cyrus. And his knowledge of astronomy is still acknowledged today as having influenced the wise men who, approximately five hundred years after his life, traveled from the East to worship the newborn King of the Jews in Bethlehem.[2] Daniel was remarkable.

If Daniel had given in to self-pity, anger, resentment, bitterness, unforgiveness, or a vengeful spirit with a "why me?" attitude toward God, I doubt we would ever have heard of him. Instead, three times a day, every day, Daniel chose to have an attitude of thanksgiving.

THINK ABOUT IT

What is your attitude? Especially when you're in "captivity"—bound in some way that restricts what you can do or where you can go or who you can be or what you can have? When God has allowed you to be in some sort of exile—cut off from friends, family, that which is familiar; when He has denied you personal wealth, health, prosperity, happiness—what is your attitude?

Eternal Fountainhead of All Blessings,

I worship You as a good, good Father. When You allow bad things to happen to me—Your child, whom You love—as I seek to live according to Your purpose, I know it's ultimately for my good and for Your glory. Your ways are not my ways. Your thoughts are higher than mine. The scope of Your love is measureless. I trust You. I lay my life down before You.

Thank You for never being neglectful or whimsical, but always attentive and intentional. Thank You for showing me that I can be confident that all things—with absolutely no exceptions—will work together for my ultimate good and Your glory.

When I'm tempted to complain, remind me that before You went to the Cross, You took the cup that represented Your death— Your blood that would be poured out—and You gave thanks! Help me to see Your glory in the darkness of pain, Your blessings in the disappointments of life.

For the glory of Your great name, Amen.

CHAPTER 8

Listening
MAKES A
DIFFERENCE

Speak, Lord, for your servant is listening.

1 SAMUEL 3:9

D aniel wrote, "I, Daniel, understood from the Scriptures, according to the word of the LORD given to Jeremiah the prophet, that the desolation of Jerusalem would last seventy years" (Daniel 9:2).

Daniel was not just reading the Scriptures, he pouring over the Scriptures. He came across a verse in Jeremiah that seemed to be illuminated. God drew Daniel's attention to a verse that had been there all along, but one that was filled with fresh meaning for him on that particular day as he listened to what God said to him through it. It was this promise he discovered during his Bible reading in Jeremiah that gave him insight into how to pray for his people. In fact, when the Heavenly messenger came to give Daniel his answer to prayer, he explained: "Daniel, I have now come to give you insight and understanding" (Daniel 9:22). The prayer Daniel prayed as a result of the insight he was given as he read God's Word was

> **God's voice is on a frequency that requires our ears to be tuned to hear it.**

specifically answered when his people were released from captivity three years later.

One morning I was reading my *Daily Light*, a small volume I have read since my mother gave me my first copy at age ten.[1] It consists of a compilation of Scriptures for both morning and evening. As I read the morning portion, verse after verse leaped up off the page, and I knew I was hearing God speaking to me. Let me explain.

I had just been in prayer, telling the Lord that I wasn't sure how much longer I could continue caring for my husband while overseeing my ministry, and now adding the writing of another book to an already full schedule. My husband's caregiving not only tied me to the house, but it increasingly became challenging because of his very fragile physical condition, his mental deterioration, and his wide emotional swings. Both of us were very tired. But this is what I seemed to hear the Lord say to me from His Word in response to my heart's cry. Listen and see if you can hear His voice: *Anne,[2] be strong . . . and work; for I am with you. . . . Be strong in the Lord and in the*

power of His might. . . . Let your hands be strong, you who have been hearing in these days these words by the mouth of the prophets (Daniel). . . . Go in this might of yours. . . . Therefore, since [you] have this ministry, as [you] have received mercy, [you] do not lose heart. . . . [Don't] grow weary while doing good, for in due season [you] shall reap if [you] do not lose heart.[3] What encouragement that gave me! What a total lift to my spirit! I knew God was giving me insight, not so much about my situation, but about myself. So I prayed His Word back to Him, claiming His power and His presence for all the responsibilities that were facing me. And God kept His Word to me, supplying everything I needed for each day.

I know that God speaks personally to us through His Word, but you and I need to learn to listen to His voice.[4] One way to listen is to pray before you read your Bible. Talk to God about what's on your heart and mind. Then open His Word and "listen" carefully for the gentle whisper of His voice.

THINK ABOUT IT

Why do you think it's hard to hear from God? Maybe the problem isn't with His voice. Maybe the problem is with your ears. It's time to make the choice to listen daily as you open your Bible and read it.

Our Father, who is in Heaven,

We worship You as the living God of Daniel. You set the heavens in place and laid the foundations of the earth.[5] In a world that changes and undulates like the surface of the sea, You and Your Word are unshaken. You are the Creator who spoke everything into existence through the power of Your Word.[6] Your thoughts are as high above our thoughts as the heavens are higher than the earth.[7] Who could know what's on Your mind and in Your heart except that You choose to reveal Yourself to us? And you have! You are Light.[8] You have made Yourself visible and knowable through the pages of our Bibles. And Your Word is our life.[9] It is eternal; it stands firm in the heavens.[10] There is no shadow of turning with You.[11] From age to age, from generation to generation, You and Your Word do not change.

Please tune my spiritual ears to hear Your gentle whisper as I read my Bible. I'm

listening. Quicken my heart at the sound of Your voice to recognize Your words as they leap off the page into my life. And then keep me, like Daniel, faithful in prayer to lay claim to what You have said.

For the glory of Your great name, Amen.

CHAPTER 9

A Daily Prayer Time MAKES A DIFFERENCE

Now when Daniel learned that the decree had been published, he went home to his upstairs room where the windows opened toward Jerusalem. Three times a day he got down on his knees and prayed, giving thanks to his God, just as he had done before.

DANIEL 6:10

There is something very special . . . very power-ful . . . very enriching . . . about establishing a daily prayer time so that prayer becomes our spiritual heartbeat as we develop a regular rhythm. A daily prayer time is one of the keys to Daniel's greatness.

Daniel's rhythm of prayer was to draw aside three times a day, every day, into an upstairs room where he could be undistracted and undisturbed.[1] Three times a day! I have struggled with just setting aside one time a day!

For years, I battled getting up early in the morning for a prayer time. I knew, and still know, that any time during the day is acceptable to God. But I couldn't seem to shake the conviction that the early-morning hours were ideal. The woman who taught me how to study and teach the Bible, Miss A. Wetherell Johnson, commented that when our prayer time is at night, it's like tuning our violins when the symphony is over. Why spend time only in the evening when you have already stumbled through your day? While it's wonderful to end our day in prayer, she urged me to pray in the morning, when the day before me was a

clean slate—a blank page that had yet to be filled in with success or failure.

I was also aware that again and again, a morning time of prayer is referred to in the Bible. Just in the Psalms alone there are repeated references.

> **A daily prayer time is the rhythm of a spiritually healthy life.**

"In the morning, O LORD, you hear my voice; in the morning I lay my requests before you and wait in expectation" (Psalm 5:3).

"I cry to you for help, O LORD; in the morning my prayer comes before you" (Psalm 88:13).

While these examples encouraged me, the one that drew me to choose an early-morning time with the Lord was not the example of David or the psalmists, but of Jesus Himself. After a pressure-packed day of intense ministry, Mark reveals, "Very early in the morning, while it was still dark, Jesus got up, left the house and went off to a solitary place, where he prayed" (Mark 1:35). I felt God was directing me to establish a prayer time in the morning.

But I'm not a morning person, I told myself. *I'm such a sleepyhead*. So, although I felt drawn to get up and

pray in the mornings, and although I felt convicted of disobedience when I slept to the last minute without getting up for prayer, I still didn't get up. I even had the audacity to tell the Lord that if He really wanted me to get up early, He could wake me up Himself. But I made no real choice to get up, and no preparations for what I would do if He did wake me up.

But I was miserable.

My solution to the struggle? I bought an alarm clock that sounded like a major seven-alarm fire when it went off and set it for thirty minutes before the time I knew I had to get up to start my day. The first morning it went off, it scared me silly. My heart was thumping out of my chest; my husband was yelling, "What in the world is that?"; and I knew there was no chance I was going to roll over and go back to sleep. I had achieved a "blanket victory"—victory over those blankets in the morning! I got up. But even when I calmed down, I was still sleepy as I went to pray. So I tried a different approach.

After setting my alarm the night before, after bounding out of bed in the morning the moment the alarm went off, after doing my stretches on the floor to loud worship

music, after walking-jogging outside for two and a half miles, after getting a triple shot of expresso in my latte at the coffeehouse, *then* I would come back for my prayer time. That worked! It still works for me today, although I no longer need an alarm to get me up. Getting up for an early-morning prayer time has become one of the joys of my life. And thirty minutes is no longer even close to being sufficient, although there are days when my obligations don't allow me to carve out more time than that. My average daily time with the Lord can stretch into hours. I love it! I can't wait to meet the Lord in my designated place at the designated time. But it began with a choice.

THINK ABOUT IT

What is hindering you from making the choice to establish a daily prayer time? Do excuses such as "I don't have time," "My family needs me," or "I've got other things to do" keep you from establishing a set time with the Lord? There is one other aspect of a daily morning prayer time

that I have learned from many, many past fail-
ures. It's so simple and practical that I'm amazed
that I didn't figure it out years and years ago. It's
this: if I am to get up earlier in the morning, I
must—it's not an option—I must choose to go to
bed earlier the night before. So I do.

Lover of my soul,

In this quiet hour, in this quiet place, I long to draw near. I long to be with You. Alone. To glimpse Your glory. To have a fresh revelation of who You are. I yearn for the day when my faith becomes sight and I see Your face. Until that day comes, draw me nearer to Your heart by Your Spirit.

Thank You for the hard lessons You have taught me when I've skipped time alone with You and found I was therefore not ready to meet the challenges or take the opportunities of the day. I confess my arrogance and ignorance that allow me to think anything or anyone is more important than spending set-aside time with You. I am sorry when I neglect our time or show up late for it. I'm embarrassed to acknowledge that, while You don't make me wait in line for the privilege of approaching Your throne, at times I have made You wait in line to be with me! I choose to make the time to draw

aside with You on a regular basis with a heart of gratitude that You have made the time to draw aside with me.

From this day forward, I make the choice to meet with You every day at _____ [a.m. or p.m.], for _____ [length of time]. My spirit is on the tiptoes of expectancy to discover the joy, the richness, the strength, the confidence, the assurance, the peace, and the knowledge that come from meeting with You on a daily basis!

For the glory of Your great name, Amen.

CHAPTER 10

Perseverance MAKES A DIFFERENCE

Do not throw away your confidence;
it will be richly rewarded. You need to
persevere so that when you have done
the will of God, you will receive what
he has promised.

HEBREWS 10:35–36

Six years after Daniel poured out his heart to God in urgent desperation for the nation of Judah, he himself went through an agonizing delay to the answer of his personal prayer. He had been given "a revelation," which is the equivalent of saying he was still reading his Bible. He knew the revelation was God's Word and that it was true, and he had enough insight to know that it involved game-changing world events (Daniel 10:1–2). But he couldn't seem to comprehend what it meant.

During three weeks of Heaven's silence, Daniel went into a form of deep spiritual depression, unable to eat or even to bathe himself. It was as though his very life depended on a deeper understanding of God's Word. But he persevered in prayer and fasting, although it wasn't easy—as indicated by the fact that during this time, he "mourned" (10:2). Then, after a delay of twenty-one days, the silence was broken. An answer was given through God's special messenger.

> **Getting a response from Heaven can be a long-distance marathon, not a sprint.**

Not all prayers are answered immediately. While there are biblical reasons for unanswered prayer, sometimes the answer is simply delayed.[1] There have been many times after intense, desperate pleading that I have not received an answer through a verse, nor am I given affirmation through a messenger. The waiting can be excruciating. I have to make the hard choice to persevere.

When we pray, we are entering into the realm of spiritual warfare with the enemy. So don't become discouraged when you lack evidence that your prayers are being answered, or moving Heaven, or changing anyone, much less a nation.

There are three things God's messenger emphasized to Daniel before he fulfilled Daniel's passionate desire for understanding, and you and I would do well to remember them as we pray, so that we, too, will be encouraged to persevere.

One: Spiritual warfare is serious.

When the messenger addressed Daniel, he instructed him, "Consider carefully the words I am about to speak to you, and stand up" (10:11).

In other words, Daniel needed to

listen up. And so do you and I. We need to pay attention, not only to God's Word, but to this very serious aspect of prayer.

Two: Spiritual warfare is subtle.

The second aspect of spiritual warfare the messenger conveyed to Daniel was subtler. It was revealed when he addressed Daniel twice with his response, "You who are highly esteemed" (10:11, 19). Did Daniel think that because his prayer had not been answered as immediately and specifically as his previous prayer had been, he had somehow fallen out of favor with God? That Heaven was no longer moved by his prayers?

Three: Spiritual warfare is invisible.

The apostle Paul alerted the Ephesian followers of Jesus that spiritual warfare is not against flesh and blood (Ephesians 6:12). You may think the real battle is with a political leader or a form of government or corporate greed or the purveyors of pornography or the abortionists or radical terrorists or the school board or the city council or whatever visible enemy you can name. But the real battle is not with any visible enemy at all. The real battle is with the *invisible* enemy. We battle "against the rulers, against

the authorities, against the powers of this dark world, and against the spiritual forces of evil in the heavenly realms"—the invisible enemy who is manipulating the visible enemies to do his wicked will.

We don't need to fight. Just take a stand on God's Word and persevere in prayer (Ephesians 6:10, 13, 14). Daniel chose to persevere until he received the answer to his prayer.

THINK ABOUT IT

What lies has the enemy been telling you? When God delays answering your prayer, do you think . . .

> that somehow prayer just doesn't work for you?
>
> that God doesn't hear your prayers?
>
> that He's too busy to be bothered with you?
>
> that you are not worth His attention?
>
> that prayer didn't work the last time, so why bother praying this time?
>
> that you're not a prayer warrior anyway?

   that the promises of God are not for you so
      don't expect Him to keep them?

   that God's going to punish you by letting you
      sit in the mess you've made?

   Or maybe you think that . . .

   you don't have enough faith.

   you haven't fasted the right way.

   you haven't used the right "formula" in
      prayer.

   you haven't humbled yourself enough.

   you haven't claimed just the right combina-
      tion of His promises.

   you haven't prayed long enough . . . or
      fervently enough . . . or specifically
      enough . . . or piously enough.

Don't succumb to the enemy's lies! Don't throw away your confidence that our God is a prayer-hearing, prayer-answering, miracle-working God! You need to make the choice and persevere!

Almighty Warrior, Lion of Judah, Captain of the Armies of Heaven,

You battled all the forces of hell and overcame! You disarmed Your enemies and made a public spectacle of them as the entire universe roared in acclamation of the Lamb of God, who is also the Lion of Judah.[2]

Open my eyes to the invisible realm.

Tear away the veil of deception that the enemy has hung over my mind and my heart.

Show me that for every aspect of Your truth, Satan has a twisted counterfeit.

Give me discernment to detect . . .

his lies in contrast to Your truth,

his suggestions in contrast to Your commands,

his temptations in contrast to Your promises,

his destruction in contrast to your salvation,

his pleasures that are fleeting,
his plans that are failing,
his purposes that are futile,
And his position that is fraudulent.

Therefore, I choose to . . .

wrap myself in the Truth of Your Word so that my thoughts, decisions, and actions are in line with what You say.

I will face the foe with nothing to protect my back because I am not turning around. I will not retreat. I will not back down. I will stand my ground, and having done all, I will keep standing firm.[3]

For the glory of Your great name, Amen.

CHAPTER 11

Desperate Prayers MAKE A DIFFERENCE

In my distress I called to the LORD;
 I called out to my God.
From his temple he heard my voice
 My cry came to his ears.

2 SAMUEL 22:7

God honors our crying out to Him when we have no one else to turn to and nowhere else to go. When we feel there is no other person who can understand our pain, God is there for us. But we have to choose to acknowledge our need of Him.

When have you been in such a hard place that you were desperate? When have you had no one to turn to? No doctor or lawyer, no friend or family member, no priest or pastor, no boss or business colleague. No one you could call for help. To be all alone in your world can be a very vulnerable and terrifying place.

Daniel was desperate. He not only fasted, but he dressed "in sackcloth" (9:3). Clothing made of sacks. Or goat's hair. Or camel's hair. No linens or silks or brocades or even cottons. Clothes that the poorest of the poor wore, signifying outwardly his inward desperation. By his very appearance, he was saying, "God, I need You. If You don't answer my prayer and keep Your promise, I have no hope. There is no one else I can turn to. My hope is in You, and in You alone."

There was no pretense or pride, no indifference or independence, no self-reliance or self-righteousness,

no Plan B if this didn't work out. There was no foreign aid to ask for, no stronger nation to appeal to, no international court to hear his grievances, no friendly military to stage a coup, no hope whatsoever anywhere in the world.

Daniel was desperate on behalf of his people. God was his only hope. If God

> **Prayerlessness is pride that says you don't need God.**

didn't deliver Daniel's people from captivity, they would not be delivered. If God did not restore them to the place of His blessing, they would not be restored. If God didn't draw them back to faith in Him, they would never experience spiritual and national revival.

Like Daniel, Dori was desperately needy. She was a woman caught up in the turmoil of the Syrian civil war.[1] She had been the privileged, almost spoiled wife of a wealthy Syrian businessman. She had lived in Damascus, shopped in Europe, and vacationed in Dubai. But then one night she had received a phone call from her brother-in-law telling her that her husband had just been arrested, and she had to immediately flee her home with her two teenage children. With tears streaming down their faces and a longing look

over their shoulders at their residential mansion, they crept through the shadows of the night as they began their sixty-five-mile journey on foot to safety. About five days later, they found themselves in a holding camp two miles short of the Syrian–Jordanian border. With no food. No running water. No toilets. On the second night in the camp, with her starving children shielding her movements from any casual observer, Dori dug under the fence, walked to the highway, and began flagging down the passing trucks, begging for food and water. Four times trucks stopped, but the drivers were interested in getting something from Dori, not giving anything to her. The fourth time she fought off a would-be rapist, another trucker saw what was happening and stopped to help. Warning her of the extreme dangers of begging on the highway, he graciously and generously gave her food and water. When she thanked him effusively, the Syrian man said, "The Lord Jesus bless you, Dori. Look to Him. He will be your shelter." Then he was gone. Dori had no idea what the man was talking about, but she felt a strange peace come into her heart as she took the food back to her children.

The next day Dori and her children climbed

under the fence and crossed the border, walking two more days to Amman. With the little bit of money she had brought with her, she was able to secure an old, rundown apartment in the center of the city. She was helped by a very kind woman who described herself as one of the "Bible people." This woman named Samar not only helped Dori and the two young people get settled in the apartment, but she explained to Dori who Jesus was when He began appearing to Dori in her dreams. Finally, Dori made the very dangerous decision to leave Islam and follow Him, knowing that her choice could cost her her life.

Several nights later, as Dori lay on the cold, hard cement floor, listening to her daughter's soft weeping and her son's grumbling, she decided to try and pray. Without doubt, Dori had never heard of Daniel, but she prayed out of desperation, *Jesus, we are so tired and hungry. We have nothing in this apartment. It's a miserable life, but I know You love us . . .* then she drifted off to sleep.

The next morning, as sunlight poured through the only window in the apartment, she was startled awake by an insistent knock at her door. Apprehensive,

she rose to answer, but her son got to the door first and opened it. A deliveryman stood at the door with his arms filled with groceries. When Dori inquired about who had sent him, he replied he didn't know. But he asked her if she needed food. When she nodded, he handed her the groceries as he explained that someone in the alley had pointed him to her apartment. Then he was gone. But first thing every morning that week, she heard a knock at her door. When she opened it, she would find a deliveryman. Never the same two men, but always different. And each one brought different things. One brought more food. Another brought clothes. Then beds and blankets. Coats and jackets. Space heaters. At the end of the week, Dori's apartment was furnished and her refrigerator was full. Because when we choose to acknowledge our need of Him, God comes through.

One thing Dori has taught me: prayer doesn't have to be fancy, or long, or filled with Bible verses. In fact, I almost wonder if it needs words at all. It really is a heart's cry.

Daniel, whose greatness bridged world empires and transcends the centuries, dressed in sackcloth. He made the choice to acknowledge he needed God.

THINK ABOUT IT

Are you embarrassed to admit your need? Do you somehow think God will blame you because you are not self-sufficient? The opposite is true. God loves to be needed. He promises to "meet all your needs according to his glorious riches in Christ Jesus" (Philippians 4:19). But you must choose to acknowledge your need and ask.

King of kings and Lord of lords,

*I bow before You. You are magnificent.
You alone are worthy of all praise and
honor and glory and power and wisdom
and wealth. You are the Source of life, the
Sustainer of life. The next breath I draw is
a gift of Your grace and mercy. How can I
begin to think that I don't need You? For
everything. For anything.*

*You have said You did not come
"to call the righteous, but sinners to
repentance" because sinners know they
need a Savior.[2] You have warned that the
attitude—even within the church—that
arrogantly refuses to acknowledge need,
boasting, "I am rich; I have acquired
wealth and do not need a thing,"[3] is
repulsive to You and will be rejected
by You.*

*So, I receive Your counsel, and come as
one who is spiritually "wretched, pitiful,
poor, blind and naked."[4] I need You. You*

have promised that if I ask in Your name, I will receive.[5]

I know I am coming to the King. Your resources are unlimited. Your grace is sufficient. Your power is undisputed. Your love is unconditional. I know I can never ask for too much. You generously give gifts both great and small. Bowing humbly before You, I ask for: _____

Before receiving it from Your hand, I thank You.

For the glory of Your great name, Amen.

CHAPTER 12

Values MAKE A DIFFERENCE

Whatever is true, whatever is noble, whatever is right, whatever is pure, whatever is lovely, whatever is admirable—if anything is excellent or praiseworthy—think about such things.

PHILIPPIANS 4:8

Although Daniel had lived in Jerusalem for approximately the first fifteen years of his life, the rest of his long life of well over eighty years was lived in Babylon. And he had not been isolated in Babylon. Like a young man thrown overboard into the sea and told to either learn to swim or drown, Daniel had been immersed in all things Babylonian. Food. Culture. Religion. Dress. Language. Politics. Government. Business practices. Education. He was saturated and brainwashed according to Nebuchadnezzar's decree. It stood to reason that in order to survive he needed to become, for all intents and purposes, Babylonian. Amazingly, he didn't. Instead, he chose to live by the values established by God and instilled in him by his parents. Values that work, as demonstrated by his life.

The experience that perhaps more than any other seems to sum up the values by which Daniel chose to live took place when Darius appointed Daniel as one of his three top officials. Daniel was so exceptional that Darius planned to make him second in command over the entire kingdom. The other rulers were

jealous and began a private investigation of Daniel in hopes of coming up with something they could smear him with, and thereby prevent his promotion by discrediting him in the eyes of the king. They found nothing . . . except that three times a day Daniel went into his upstairs room, opened his window toward Jerusalem, and prayed. Although that seemed very small and insignificant, it was enough to give them ammunition against him.

The rulers went to Darius with smooth, flattering words and convinced him to issue a decree that people could pray only to him and to no other god. The obviously egotistical Darius agreed. Being fed to starving lions would be the penalty for disobedience. The horror of such a death would surely be a strong deterrent against looking to any god besides Darius.

> **Values that are worth living by are worth dying for.**

Daniel was aware of the decree, but he didn't flinch. There was not a stutter in his step as he climbed to his upstairs room. He did not even close his shutters so he could pray unobserved. Instead, as always, he opened his window toward Jerusalem and

continued praying three times a day. Sure enough, his enemies were lurking in the shadows. They saw him in prayer and ran gleefully to report to the king.

The king was genuinely distressed because Daniel held great favor in his estimation. Though the king's eyes were opened to the plot, it was too late to do anything about it. The law he had signed into effect was the law of the Medes and Persians. It was irrevocable. So Daniel, the great man of God who had served Babylon and then Persia with such exceptional distinction, was thrown into the lions' den as the king himself uttered a type of prayer: "May your God, whom you serve continually, rescue you!" (Daniel 6:16). The king himself seemed to have "caught" Daniel's bold, confident faith, because faith is contagious, remember?

Darius tossed and turned all night. He could not eat and he could not sleep. Early the next morning, he ran to the lions' den, calling out, "'Daniel, servant of the living God, has your God, whom you serve continually, been able to rescue you from the lions?' Daniel answered, 'O king, live forever!

My God sent his angel, and he shut the mouths of the lions. They have not hurt me'" (6:20–22).

The overjoyed Darius pulled Daniel up out of the den and then immediately executed the men who had hatched the plot against him. The king then decreed that everyone in his kingdom was to fear and revere the God of Daniel. Listen to Darius's testimony: "For he is the living God and he endures forever; his kingdom will not be destroyed, his dominion will never end" (6:26).

Daniel chose to remain true to his values, and therefore God was glorified by the four world emperors under whom he served!

THINK ABOUT IT

What are your values? What principle . . . what truth . . . what ideology or philosophy . . . what faith . . . would you be willing to die for?

Blessed Lord Jesus,

You are the pearl of great price. You are the summation of every value worth knowing and keeping and living by and dying for. We would gladly sell all of our treasure for the highest privilege of knowing You. We worship You as One who got up from Heaven's throne, took off Your glory robes, made Yourself nothing, took on the form of a servant, humbled Yourself, and became obedient even to death. You willingly flung Yourself into the "lions' den" of Satanic activity, with the furnace of hell's fury heated seven times hotter, in order to be true to the purpose for which You had been born. And the Father sent no angels to stay the hand of the executioners. Instead, You were nailed to a Roman cross and hung out to die. You gave Your life for me.

How can I say thank You? Words are too small, too inadequate to express my gratitude. And so I choose to lay my life

down for You, knowing that living for You may require more effort and discipline than dying for You.

Help me to be true to the values You taught and exemplified: humility, integrity, purity, sincerity, loyalty, charity, to name just a few. I want to be like You in all things.

For the glory of Your great name, Amen.

CHAPTER 13

Focus MAKES A DIFFERENCE

Let us fix our eyes on Jesus, the author and perfecter of our faith, who for the joy set before him endured the cross, scorning its shame, and sat down at the right hand of the throne of God.

HEBREWS 12:2

Jesus said, "The eye is the lamp of the body. If your eyes are good, your whole body will be full of light. But if your eyes are bad, your whole body will be full of darkness. If then the light within you is darkness, how great is that darkness!" (Matthew 6:22–23).

Let's exchange the word "eye" for "focus," and the word "body" for "life" in the above passage. Now what Jesus said reads like this: "The focus is the lamp of the life. If your focus is good, your whole life will be full of light. But if your focus is bad, your whole life will be full of darkness."

The focus of your life determines your priorities and your loyalties. If the focus of your life is off—if it is anything other than pleasing and glorifying God—then the light within you is darkness! Jesus went on to explain, "No one can serve two masters. Either he will hate the one and love the other, or he will be devoted to the one and despise the other" (Matthew 6:24). You can't be divided in your focus or you will become cross-eyed and your perspective on life will become blurry.

This clarity of focus can easily be seen in the choice Daniel's three friends made. Like Daniel, Meshach, Shadrach, and Abednego were also captured

in Jerusalem and enslaved with him in Babylon. They, too, had refused the king's food, eaten the alternative diet, and like Daniel, had been found to be superior to the captives who compromised. As a result, they, too, had entered the king's service, and after Daniel interpreted the king's dream, they had been elevated to administrative leadership in the province.

Shortly thereafter, the king issued a proclamation requiring all of his officials throughout Babylon to come to the plain of Shinar. Since Daniel had been assigned to the royal court, he was exempt from the king's edict. But his three friends were

> **Clarity of focus keeps us from stumbling around in a twilight zone.**

required to attend the official dedication of a gold-plated, ninety-foot-tall replica of Nebuchadnezzar. While it was just a wooden pole overlaid with gold, on the flat plain it must have looked like the new One World Trade Center in Lower Manhattan.

Once all the Babylonian officials had gathered, they were informed that when they heard the band strike up, they were to fall down and worship the image of gold. If they did not, they would be thrown

into a furnace of fire. When the music began, people as far as the eye could see fell prostrate. When the movement of the people grew still, the strains of the music wafted through the dusty air, and it was apparent that everyone had complied—everyone except three young Hebrew men who remained ramrod straight.

Immediately someone informed the king of their insubordination. They were arrested and taken before Nebuchadnezzar who was "furious with rage" (Daniel 3:13). He told them he would give them one more chance to bow down. If they did not, they would be burned alive because "what god will be able to rescue you from my hand?" (3:15).

Their response was an expression of confident faith that was laser focused: "O Nebuchadnezzar, we do not need to defend ourselves before you in this matter. If we are thrown into the blazing furnace, the God we serve is able to save us from it, and he will rescue us from your hand, O king. But even if he does not, we want you to know, O king, that we will not serve your gods or worship the image of gold you have set up" (3:16–18). In other words, they would rather be burned alive than risk displeasing or dishonoring their God.

The king was furious. Although he had recognized them earlier as three of the best and brightest of his captives, and although he had placed them in prominent positions of leadership, the Bible records that his attitude toward the three young men changed. He ordered the furnace heated seven times hotter than usual; commanded his strongest soldiers to tie them up fully clothed with robes, trousers, and turbans; and then had the three young men thrown into the fire. The flames were so intense that they incinerated the men who threw Meshach, Shadrach, and Abednego into the furnace.

Expecting to see the young men quickly burned to a crisp, Nebuchadnezzar instead jumped up out of his seat and demanded of his guards, "Weren't there three men that we tied up and threw into the fire? . . . Look! I see four men walking around in the fire, unbound and unharmed, and the fourth looks like a son of the gods" (3:24–25). God Himself had shown up! He walked in the midst of the fire with His children. Because, remember? God honors those who honor Him.

With a dramatically different tone to his voice, the king respectfully asked the young men to step out of the furnace. When they did, everyone gathered around to touch, to look, to sniff, and to thoroughly examine them, but they found that not even one hair of their heads was singed. Their robes had no smell of fire or smoke. Even Nebuchadnezzar knew he had witnessed a miraculous intervention of the one true living God. He responded with, "Praise be to the God of Shadrach, Meshach, and Abednego who has sent his angel and rescued his servants!" (3:28).

Once again, because these three young men chose to stay focused on God, He was glorified and they were honored with promotions in their positions of service.

Meshach, Shadrach, and Abednego chose to stay focused, even in the midst of the flames.

THINK ABOUT IT

What is the real focus of your life? Examine what consumes your thoughts and how you spend the majority of your time and your money. You may be surprised at how cross-eyed you are.

Beloved Lord Jesus of Nazareth,

We worship You as One who set Your face "like a flint" (Isaiah 50:7 NKJV). You remained focused on Your Father's will until You completed it (John 17:4). We have heard Your victory shout reverberate from the Cross, "It is finished!" (John 19:30 NKJV). We know Your victory was not an accident. You achieved it because You lived Your life every moment—twenty-four, seven—intentionally focused on how You spent Your time, the words You spoke, the people You were with, the places You went. As a result, Your Father was glorified (John 17:4)!

Your Word challenges us, as Your followers, to "fix our eyes on Jesus, the author and perfecter of our faith, who for the joy set before him endured the cross, scorning its shame, and sat down at the right hand of the throne of God. Consider him . . ." (Hebrews 12:2–3). You are the One with eyes of omniscience who looked

down the centuries until Your focus rested on me. I was the "joy" that helped You endure the Cross that my sin made necessary.

Please, take my face in Your hands. Turn my eyes upon You. Keep me focused on You in all that I say and do until my focus becomes crystal clear when my faith becomes sight and I see You face-to-face.

For the glory of Your great name, Amen.

CHAPTER 14

Courage
MAKES A
DIFFERENCE

For God did not give us a spirit of
timidity, but a spirit of power, of love
and of self-discipline. So do not be
ashamed to testify about our Lord.

2 TIMOTHY 1:7–8

Daniel had been in Babylon for decades when we are told of a very dramatic confrontation he had with the new king, Nebuchadnezzar's spoiled successor, Belshazzar.

With the Medo-Persian army laying siege outside the walls of the city of Babylon, Belshazzar decided to throw a party for the officials of his kingdom. It doesn't take much imagination to describe the scene of opulence. Lavish food, free-flowing wine, provocative entertainment, and powerful men being seduced by beautiful women led to everyone becoming intoxicated and all restraints abandoned.

It was then that Belshazzar stepped over the line. He ordered that the golden vessels Nebuchadnezzar had seized from the temple in Jerusalem—the vessels that had been used in worship of the one, true living God of Abraham, Isaac, and Jacob—be brought into the banqueting hall. He then passed them around to his drunken friends and used them to toast Babylon's pagan gods.

At that moment, the fingers of a mysterious hand without an arm appeared and wrote something on the

wall. "The king watched the hand as it wrote. His face turned pale and he was so frightened that his knees knocked together and his legs gave way" (Daniel 5:5–6).

The silence must have been deafening as all merriment and movement ceased. The king was suddenly stone cold sober and terrified, shaking from limb to limb. He called for his wise men to come in and interpret the writing, promising that whoever could read it and interpret it would be clothed in purple, have a gold chain placed around his neck, and be promoted to third highest ruler in Babylon. But even with those generous incentives, no one could even guess what the strange script was about, much less read and accurately interpret it.

At that point, there must have been an outbreak of curses, shouting, threats, and general confusion because the queen mother heard the commotion and came into the banquet hall. And this is what she said: "Don't be alarmed!

> **Courage is the fruit of deeply held conviction.**

Don't look so pale! There is a man in your kingdom who has the spirit of the holy gods in him. In the time

of your father he was found to have insight and intelligence and wisdom like that of the gods. . . . Call for Daniel, and he will tell you what the writing means" (5:10–12).

So the king sent for Daniel. What a contrast to all the wealthy, spoiled, drunken, baffled officials Daniel must have been with his dignity and humility. He would have been an old man by then with the deep etchings of godly character in his face. I would imagine that he held his head high, with a fearlessness in his eyes that would have made the king shudder in his miserable spirit.

The king addressed Daniel with disrespectful, condescending words that surely were intended to put him in his place, remind him of his inferior position, and intimidate him into submission. "Are you Daniel, one of the exiles my father the king brought from Judah?" (5:13). In other words, "You're a nobody. Captured. Enslaved." He went on to say, "But I've heard you are smart and can solve difficult problems. If you can solve this one, I will clothe you in purple, put a gold chain around your neck, and make

you the third highest ruler in Babylon" (paraphrase of 5:14–16).

To Daniel's credit, he didn't laugh in the king's face. But he also didn't hesitate. He courageously responded, "You may keep your gifts for yourself and give your rewards to someone else" (5:17). Then he proceeded to unleash the full warning of God's judgment because of the king's arrogant, willful, and wicked ways. "You did not honor the God who holds in his hand your life," he accused (5:23). And then Daniel read him the riot act—the handwriting that was on the wall: "God has numbered the days of your reign and brought it to an end. . . . You have been weighed on the scales and found wanting. . . . Your kingdom is divided and given to the Medes and Persians" (5:26–28).

Even as Daniel spoke, the Medes and Persians slipped under the gate of the city, and by morning, Belshazzar was dead and his kingdom had passed to Darius.

Daniel chose to be courageous because he was convinced of the truth and the solid belief that there is a Higher Authority who determines future destinies.

THINK ABOUT IT

In our politically correct culture, how convinced of the truth are you? Are you so convinced that you will choose to courageously proclaim it regardless of the consequences, confident it comes from One with supreme authority?

Son of God and Son of Man,

We worship You as One who had all power and authority in the universe—One who was worshipped and adored—yet made the courageous choice to get up from Your throne, take off Your glory robes, and humble Yourself in order to take on human flesh, entering time and space as a baby. In You we behold the glory of God, full of grace and truth.

What courage it must have required to grow in wisdom and stature and in favor with God and man, yet be rejected by those You had come to save.

What courage it must have demanded to love those who were Your enemies, and in the end, submit to their cruelty.

But the choice that was the most courageous of all . . . the choice that's beyond human comprehension . . . was Your choice to go to the Cross and stay on the Cross until in the end You refused to

take another breath and gave Your life on the Cross as God's sacrifice for sin.

Thank You for loving me when I was still a sinner and didn't even know I needed You. Thank You for giving Your life for me.

Now it's my turn. In gratitude, I choose courage as I give my life to You. Help me live courageously—and even confront when necessary—with dignity, nobility, clarity, and integrity as I stand firmly on the Foundation of Truth that will never be moved.

For the glory of Your great name, Amen.

CHAPTER 15

Confession
MAKES A
DIFFERENCE

If we confess our sins, he is
faithful and just and will forgive
us our sins and purify us from all
unrighteousness.

1 JOHN 1:9

Daniel testified that God's answer to his prayer came "while I was speaking and praying, confessing my sin and the sin of my people" (9:20). When was the last time you confessed your sin? I've found that I tend to be so superficial spiritually that at times I'm not aware that I have sinned.

One of my more painful experiences took place before leading a seminar several years ago. I had set aside ten days to work on the seven different messages I would be giving. On the first day, I pulled out my Bible, my pencil, and my legal pad; said a quick prayer asking for God's blessing; and then began to work through the passage of Scripture that would be the basis for the first message. As I sought to break open the passage, I got nothing. No real revelation or understanding at all. I knew I was just spinning my mental and spiritual wheels, so I

The ground is level at the foot of the Cross.

concluded that my weariness was dulling my mind. I decided to put myself to bed with the intention of

beginning in the morning when I felt more alert and fresh.

The next morning, after a good night's sleep, a brisk walk and a substantial breakfast, I felt refreshed. So I sat down at my desk where my Bible was still open from the night before, picked up my pen, and held it poised over the legal pad to begin writing my first thoughts. Once again I prayed, this time with more expectancy. I then proceeded to read and reread the passage of Scripture. Nothing.

I prayed again, except this time there was an insistent edge to my prayer as I explained to the Lord that I only had a limited time to prepare the messages, that hundreds of people who had paid to hear them would be arriving within nine days, and that I needed His help. Nothing.

And then, there seemed to be a small whisper in my heart. *Anne, I don't want to talk about the messages. I want to talk about you.* Recognizing the still, small voice of the Spirit, I replied honestly, *I don't want to talk about me. There's no time. I want to talk about these messages. After I have prepared and delivered them, then we will talk about me.*

Nothing.

Only now there was dead silence that was becoming quite loud. With a panicked pace to my heart, I pondered what was going on. I knew there was no way I could prepare the messages without His help, so the only option I could come up with was to talk about what He wanted to talk about. As quickly as I could.

I got down on my knees, and I admit there were tears on my face as I asked Him what He wanted to talk about. I was listening. Five days later, He was still talking. About sin! In my life! Every time I opened my Bible a verse seemed to leap up off the page, indicting me for another sin I hadn't been aware of. It was awful. Painful. Humiliating. To the extreme.

This dialogue with a very holy God was triggered by a little book I was reading by an old-timey revivalist.[1] The third chapter was entitled, "Preparing the Heart for Revival," and it was based on Hosea 10:12: "Break up your unplowed ground; for it is time to seek the Lord, until he comes and showers righteousness on you."

The author explained that to experience revival, we must look to our own hearts and the spiritual ground that has perhaps become hardened over time.

We must examine the state of our own minds and reflect on our past actions. He cautioned that he did not mean we were to glance at things, then make a general confession to God the way many of us do, with a, "Dear God, forgive me for all my many sins. Amen." Instead, he challenged the reader to take pen and paper and write down each sin as it comes to mind. Because our sins are committed one at a time, he said they must be reviewed and repented of one by one. And so I did as he said. It was like having a spiritual angiogram. Altogether, my time of conviction, confession, and cleansing lasted seven days!

God took seven days to clean me up. Seven days to point out sin I didn't even know I had. I had not been neglecting my daily Bible reading or prayer previously. I was deeply involved in studying, applying, and living out God's Word to the best of my ability. I was committed to sharing it with others. In fact, I had devoted most of my adult life to serving God outside of my home. How could I have allowed the sin to pile up like that in my heart and life? I was deeply ashamed. Humiliated before God.

In fact, I think one reason some of

us, myself included, don't examine our hearts for sin is because we are so afraid we will find it. One thing I have discovered is that it takes courage to look deep within to see what God sees. It's painful to acknowledge that we're not as good, righteous, pure, or holy as we thought we were.

For seven days, I clung to the old rugged Cross. I discovered in a fresh, very personal way that the blood of Jesus is not just for unsaved sinners who come to the Cross for the first time, but for saved sinners who need to come back and back and back. Praise God! The blood of Jesus never runs out. It never loses its power to cleanse and to wash us as white as snow. *I know . . .*

Looking back, I now know that what I had experienced was revival. Personal revival. It's what I have longed to see take place corporately so that the entire church is revived and our nation is restored.

Which leads me back to Daniel. I am convinced that the key to revival is repentance. And that the key to repentance is prayer. Not prayer that preaches at people. But prayer that comes out of our own hearts, broken for our own sin.

THINK ABOUT IT

Are you courageous enough to take a pencil and paper in hand to write down the sins you see in yourself? Confess your sins. Tell God you're sorry. Ask Him to cleanse you of all of them. Ask Him not to miss anything in your heart, mind, or life that needs the blood of Jesus. Do it now. Take as long as you need. Seven minutes, seven hours, seven days, seven weeks, seven months. Just do it. As we pray for revival, ask Him to let it begin with you.

Most Holy Lord,

You have "clothed me with the garments of salvation and arrayed me in a robe of [Your] righteousness . . . as a bride adorns herself with her jewels."[2]

But in my Christian walk I am still in rags;

My best prayers are stained with sin;

My penitential tears are muddied with self.

I need to repent of my repentance;

I need my tears to be washed . . .

I have sinned times without number,

And been guilty of pride and unbelief,

Of failure to find Thy mind in Thy Word,

Of neglect to seek Thee in my daily life.

I confess . . .

I am so slow to learn,

So prone to forget

Too weak to climb;

Destroy in me every lofty thought,

Break pride to pieces and scatter it to the winds,

Annihilate each clinging shred of self-righteousness,

Implant in me true lowliness of spirit . . .

Open in me a fount of penitential tears,

Break me, then bind me up. [3]

For the glory of Your great name, Amen.

CHAPTER 16

Fasting MAKES A DIFFERENCE

When you fast . . .

MATTHEW 6:16

Have you ever fasted? From anything? One key to Daniel's powerful and effective prayer is that he chose to fast. Daniel "turned to the Lord God and pleaded with him . . . in fasting" (Daniel 9:3).

Fasting simply means to go without anything and everything to make time to pray. We associate it most often with abstaining from food, but it can also be abstinence from business, emails, phone calls, ministry, entertainment, web surfing, meetings, housework, shopping, cooking, talking, television, technology—the list is unlimited. While in prayer, we *turn to God*; in fasting we *turn away* from everything else.

We don't fast to show God how pious we are. He already knows. It is not a "work" we are to add to our prayer effort to merit His answer. His answers are gifts of His grace, not rewards for our work. It is not to make God love us more or pay us more attention. He loves us completely, fully. He can't love us any more. And He has already

> **It's time to go on a spiritual diet and fast.**

given us His undivided attention without our fasting. So why do we fast?

One reason is because Jesus expects us to fast. He told His disciples, "*When* you fast . . ." (Matthew 6:16, emphasis added). Not *if* you fast. For me, fasting has helped to purify my motives in prayer. It sharpens my focus on heavenly things and clarifies my perspective on earthly things. It prompts me to pray more persistently and frequently. And perhaps most importantly, fasting reveals to me how sincere I really am as I seek the Lord in prayer.

I first discovered the power of fasting when my husband, Danny, and I were newly married. We enjoyed just being together for a while, but then came the day when we decided we wanted children. In my naïveté, I thought all I had to do was to stop using birth control and babies would start coming. I was wrong. Month after month, my womb would empty out. I went to specialists who assured me nothing was wrong, but they couldn't tell me why I did not get pregnant.

I shared my grief with my very wise mother, who responded, "Anne, if more mothers prayed for their babies like

Hannah prayed for hers, maybe we would have more Samuels." So I turned in my Bible and read about Hannah to learn what was so unique about her prayer life (1 Samuel 1). I discovered that she was greatly beloved by her husband, whose only words of comfort to her were that she ought to consider him better to her than ten sons. But a husband—even a loving husband—was no substitute for a baby. She knew that, and so did I. Hannah wanted her own baby with such intensity that she wept and could no longer eat. She fasted from food. Then she fasted from everything when she went up to the temple to pray.

In answer to her prayer and fasting, God promised her a son. Soon after, she became pregnant and gave birth to Samuel, a little boy that she dedicated to God. Samuel grew "in stature and in favor with the LORD and with men" (1 Samuel 2:26), becoming an exceedingly great man who was a prophet, judge, and kingmaker in Israel.

Following Hannah's example, I set aside one day each week to pray and fast for a son. One year after I turned to the Lord with fasting on a regular, weekly basis, I seemed to hear God whispering to my heart, *Anne, you don't have to fast anymore. I will give you a*

baby. You will have a son. I immediately stopped fasting and instead, started praising God for having heard and answered my prayer. The next month, I conceived a baby. Nine months later, I gave birth to our son, Jonathan.

Was I able to get pregnant and give birth to Jonathan because I had fasted? I honestly don't know. What I do know is that fasting changed me. By the end of that year of prayer and fasting, I was genuinely, sincerely satisfied with the Lord and with my husband. If I had not gotten pregnant, if I had never had any children at all, I knew I would be okay. Interestingly, it was when I let go and released my desire for a baby that I became pregnant. So indirectly, fasting seemed to make a difference, because without it I don't believe I would have been able to release my all-consuming passionate desire for a child.

THINK ABOUT IT

What has you so absorbed that you can't turn away from it mentally, emotionally, and/or

spiritually? That's one reason you need to fast—to break the consuming preoccupation with anything other than the kingdom of God and His righteousness—first. I suggest that you choose to build fasting into your prayer life, if you haven't already. Talk to God about it; then decide what you will fast from, when you will fast from it, and how long you will maintain your fast. Then do it. Discover for yourself the difference it makes.

Lord God Almighty,

We worship You as One who sits enthroned above all. Your authority extends to every corner of the universe. Your Word is true. What You say is so. We choose not to "fear those who kill the body but cannot kill the soul. But rather [we] fear Him who is able to destroy both soul and body in hell" (Matthew 10:28 NKJV).

Thank You that You are God. And You are our God. We don't have to be afraid or intimidated by earthly leaders who reject, despise, and blaspheme Your name while wielding their temporary, limited, earthly authority. Yet in our frail flesh, we will be intimidated and afraid unless we choose to focus on You, and You alone.

Thank You for giving us the spiritual discipline of fasting to help us be more aware of Your presence than that of other people. To care more about what You think than what others think. To trust Your

Word when it's contradicted by the culture or our circumstances.

To strengthen my spiritual core, I choose to fast—to draw aside and give You my undivided attention.

For the glory of Your great name, Amen.

CHAPTER 17

Forgiveness MAKES A DIFFERENCE

Bear with each other and forgive whatever grievances you may have against one another. Forgive as the Lord forgave you.

COLOSSIANS 3:13

The Bible doesn't tell us if Daniel struggled with forgiving those who inflicted pain in his life: betrayal, injustice, unfairness, slander, accusations, and even persecution. The list would have been a lengthy one that surely would have included Nebuchadnezzar, who had captured and enslaved him, killing many of his friends, neighbors, and perhaps even his family members in Jerusalem; cruel guards; jealous coworkers; resentful born-and-bred Babylonians. But Daniel must have made the choice to forgive, and then lived in that forgiveness.

Forgiveness is *not* pretending that I have not been hurt, or saying that what the other person did was not wrong. It is not letting my offender "get by with it" by not holding him or her accountable.

I've learned that forgiveness is an intellectual choice I am commanded to make. If it were a feeling or an emotion, I couldn't obey the command since I can't necessarily control my emotions and feelings. It's a choice, pure and simple. If I only offered forgiveness to those who ask for it, or those who deserve it, or those I feel like forgiving, there are some people

I would never forgive. But it's a decision that I make because I am commanded to forgive for one very simple reason: God has forgiven me (Ephesians 4:32; see also Matthew 6:15). As an act of grateful worship, I choose to forgive others.

But my decision to forgive needs to be followed with an act of love that's sacrificial in nature. I need to do something for the person I am forgiving—something that is costly. Something I would do for no other reason than that it's my act of worship—worship of the One who laid down His life for me as His own act of sacrificial, loving forgiveness.

I have a dear friend, Barb,[1] whose mother had never ceased to find fault with her. Ever since Barb was a little girl, her mother criticized everything she did. Barb told me that months before Christmas every year, she began to

> **Refusing to forgive is like drinking poison and hoping the other person will die.**

feel nauseated because selecting the expected gift was so traumatic. It didn't matter what the gift was, her mother would not be pleased. Barb dreaded Christmas for that reason alone.

Barb and her mother were involved with other

family members in a business venture. One particular year, Barb's mother actually took out a lawsuit against her involving the business. At the same time, the older woman was moving out of the home she'd had for decades and into a condominium—and Barb was helping her move! As if that weren't enough, Barb was a fabulous seamstress, and she sewed the drapes and other things for her mother's new home.

Barb had dropped by my house one morning, and I remember looking incredulously at her. She was standing on my front steps when I challenged her bluntly, "Barb, how can you do it? How in the world can you help your mother, sew for her, do all these other things, while she is suing you in court?" I will never forget Barb's response. She taught me a life lesson that I've been able to share with others.

"Anne, I've chosen to forgive my mother," she replied. "But I have to tell you, every time my mother comes to mind, every time I see her or hear the sound of her voice, I have to forgive her all over again. Jesus has taught me to forgive seventy times seven [see Matthew 18:22 NKJV]—to place no limits on my forgiveness. But when I made the choice to forgive her, I also made the decision to love her sacrificially. Helping her is my

way of showing her I've forgiven her and that I love her. And actually, it has helped me let go. I have been set free from bitterness, anger, and resentment." I looked at Barb's gentle expression, the light of joy in her eyes, and I knew she was speaking the truth. She was free— free to forgive, free to love.

Don't underestimate the power of forgiveness in your own life. While others may remain distant, hardened, cold, and vengeful, and respond negatively to your forgiveness—if they respond at all—the very act of forgiveness fleshed out in sacrificial love will begin the healing process *in you.* And sometimes it does make a difference in the other person.

Although there was no evidence at the time, Barb's forgiveness and love softened her mother's heart. As Barb chose to move forward, within a few years, she had the privilege of leading her mother to receive God's love by placing her faith in Jesus Christ for her own forgiveness. Shortly thereafter, her mother stepped into eternity. The sting of her mother's death and the victory of the grave were removed as a result of the powerful choice Barb had made to forgive.[2]

What difference will forgiveness make? You won't know until you choose to forgive.

THINK ABOUT IT

Is your life on the verge of being mired in the quicksand of your past? If you were to come under scrutiny, as Daniel did, would there be little cobwebs of unforgiveness, bitterness, and resentment deep in the recesses of your heart, pulling you down? Isn't it time you turned everything over to the One who said, "Vengeance is Mine, I will repay" (Romans 12:19 NKJV)?

Trust God to sort things out. He is the Judge who will make it right in the end. In the meantime, you are free to love.

Gracious Redeemer,

Before Your Cross I kneel and see the heinousness of my sin, my iniquity that caused You to be "made a curse," the evil that excites the severity of divine wrath.

Show me the enormity of my guilt by the crown of thorns, the pierced hands and feet, the bruised body, the dying cries.

Your blood is the blood of incarnate God, its worth infinite, its value beyond all thought.

Infinite must be the evil and guilt that demand such a price . . .

Yet Your compassions yearn over me, Your heart hastens to my rescue, Your love endured my curse, Your mercy bore my deserved stripes.[3]

I kneel before You, a sinner saved from God's wrath by Your grace. Absolved of all my guilt. I am forgiven of all my sin. Past, present, and future. Redeemed by Your blood—the blood of God's Lamb! I am forgiven! I am forgiven! Hallelujah! I am

*forgiven! How could I then ever withhold
my forgiveness from someone else?*

*In expression of my worship of You, I
forgive others as I have been forgiven.*

*For the glory of Your great name,
Amen.*

CHAPTER 18

Humility
MAKES A
DIFFERENCE

Humble yourselves before the Lord,
and he will lift you up.

JAMES 4:10

Daniel was a man God highly esteemed. As we have already seen, he had entered Babylon as a slave. While he remained a slave all of his life, he had quickly risen through the ranks of officials in Nebuchadnezzar's court until he was ruler over Babylon (Daniel 2:48). Daniel held this high position under three more emperors in three successive empires: Belshazzar, who briefly ruled in Babylon; Darius, who destroyed the Babylonians and ushered in the Medo-Persian Empire; and finally Cyrus, who eliminated the Medes and set up the Persian Empire. In anyone and everyone's estimation, Daniel was a very great, important, powerful man.

Daniel was lavishly honored by kings for his almost unlimited supernatural wisdom. God revealed to Daniel the dreams of others, as well as what the dreams meant. Angels personally delivered God's answers to Daniel's prayers. And God miraculously delivered him when his enemies had contrived to have him fed to lions. It was obvious that he was a very great, important, powerful man in Heaven's estimation, too.

Daniel was also a prophet in the Old Testament who is considered the equivalent to the apostle John in the New Testament. The 100 percent historical accuracy of his predictions has been phenomenal. For this reason, his insight into the world from his day until the end of time is still endlessly studied by scholars and theologians who consider him to be a great man by modern standards.

Daniel, whose greatness bridged world empires and transcends the centuries, who had every human "right" to think very highly of himself, didn't. As he

The way up is down.

began to pray, he smeared himself with "ashes" (9:3). He deliberately, intentionally made the choice to humble himself.

Jesus told a parable to those "who were confident of their own righteousness and looked down on everybody else" (Luke 18:9). He described two men who went up to the temple to pray.[1] One was a Pharisee, a highly educated leader in Israel who was so scrupulous in the way he kept all the nuances, regulations, and traditions of his religion that he was considered exemplary. The other was a tax collector

who was considered a "low-life" because, although a Jew, he collaborated with the occupying Romans for pay. Most tax collectors were also cheats and were despised by "good" people as sinners.

So Jesus described these two men from God's perspective. The Pharisee "stood up and prayed about himself" saying, "God, I thank you that I am not like all other men . . . or even like this tax collector. I fast twice a week and give a tenth of all I get." Then Jesus contrasted the Pharisee with His description of the tax collector who "stood at a distance. He would not even look up to heaven, but beat his breast and said, 'God have mercy on me, a sinner'" (Luke 18:11–13).

In the event that someone listening didn't understand His meaning, Jesus summarized His story, "I tell you that this man [the tax collector], rather than the other [the Pharisee], went home justified before God. For everyone who exalts himself will be humbled, and he who humbles himself will be exalted" (18:14). God is not impressed at all with our reputations . . . who we think we are or who others think we are. He looks on the heart. In case there is any doubt, Proverbs clearly states, "The

LORD detests all the proud of heart" (Proverbs 16:5). On the other hand, God confirms, "This is the one I esteem: he who is humble and contrite in spirit, and trembles at my word" (Isaiah 66:2). Humility matters to God.

THINK ABOUT IT

Do you think if you keep all the "rules"—if you're good, moral, helpful, thoughtful—then somehow God owes you the answer you want? Could it be that there is pride lurking like a cobweb in the dark inner recesses of your heart? Pride that suggests that you deserve not only an answer, but that you know better than God which answers He should provide! Maybe it's time for a humility heart check.

Enthroned Living Lord . . .

Everything revolves around You. Everything.

How could we have become so out of focus? Our distorted perspective is first rooted in our hearts, then reflected in our prayers. Because . . .

> *what we have wanted seems so vital;*
> *what we have thought seems so critical;*
> *what we have felt seems so crucial;*
> *what we have said sounds so spiritual;*
> *we seem to be consumed with*

ourselves!

We are so ashamed. In the light of who You are, we now get it. We understand that it's what You want that is vital, what You think that is so critical, what You feel that is crucial, what You say is the wisdom of the ages expressed in unvarnished, eternal truth. How could we have set ourselves up as gods, and expected You to fall in line with us as though You exist for our personal benefit?

Now, in the privacy of this place, I choose to humble myself. I plead with You for what You have purposed to give, for what You have wanted to do, for what You have promised to fulfill in Your Word. I want Your kingdom to come, Your will to be done on earth as it is in Heaven. I want to be a part of what You are doing . . . to come alongside You as You accomplish Your agenda.

For the glory of Your great name, Amen.

CHAPTER 19

A Personal Relationship with God MAKES A DIFFERENCE

"I am God Almighty; walk before me
and be blameless. I will confirm my
covenant between me and you."

GENESIS 17:1–2

Daniel would have entered into a covenant relationship with God as a result of growing up as a Jewish boy. The covenant was claimed by his parents, who would have had him circumcised on the eighth day of his life as an outward sign of their agreement. Daniel's willing participation in the sacrificial system and the ceremonies in the temple further solidified his relationship with God. Even in his old age, his memories of the temple sacrifices were precious to him, because his participation had been heartfelt, not just ritualistic or traditional (see Daniel 9:21). He knew the living God was his God. When God came through for him as Daniel chose again and again to trust Him completely under great pressure and at great risk to himself, he became increasingly confident that God had claimed him also.

I know that I am in a covenant relationship with God, too. As I related in an earlier chapter, my confidence is based on the choice I made when I was eight or nine and I confessed my sin, asked God to forgive me, and placed

my trust in Jesus as my Savior and Lord. Although with my child's mind I didn't understand at the time, looking back, I now know that's when I entered into a covenant relationship with God.

Jesus explained this covenant on the night He was betrayed, when He instituted an ordinance with His disciples that we keep today and refer to as Holy Communion. After

> God has no back-room, smoke-and-mirrors, clandestine relationships.

His last supper before His death on the Cross, He took an ordinary loaf of bread, broke it, and gave each of His disciples a piece as He explained that it represented His body, which would be broken for them. In the same manner, He took the cup of wine on the table, gave them each a sip, and expanded His explanation slightly, saying it represented His blood of the new covenant that would be poured out for the forgiveness of their sin (Luke 22:19–20; 1 Corinthians 11:23–26).

A covenant is a legal agreement between two or more parties, as in a treaty between nations. Or a land covenant between the buyer and the seller. Or a marriage covenant between husband and wife. The old

biblical covenant with God is the one Daniel entered into through the Jewish laws, ceremonies, and sacrifices. The new covenant I entered into is one that Jesus established by fulfilling the old covenant perfectly through His life and death. I entered into the new covenant as I "drank the cup" of His blood when I claimed His sacrifice on the Cross to make atonement for my sin. I "ate the bread" of His body when I took Him into my heart and gave Him access to every part of my life. The incredible, glorious truth is that once I entered into a covenant relationship with Him, He entered into that relationship with me, and I am His. Forever.

A covenant relationship with God is the equivalent of a legal promise to which He binds Himself so that you and I can take Him at His word with absolute confidence. It's His guarantee. Signed with His own blood.

And that covenant relationship with God is your choice.

THINK ABOUT IT

When have you made the choice to enter into a covenant with God? Don't assume that you have. Don't hope that you have. Don't think that you have. You can *know* that you have. If you are not sure . . . if there is any doubt whatsoever that you are in a covenant relationship with God, make sure. Right now. Confess your sins. Ask for forgiveness and for cleansing. Accept Jesus' gift of salvation. Then commit to living the rest of your life for Him—in covenant with Him.

Dear Lord God of Daniel and Father of Jesus Christ,

I worship You as a covenant-keeping God. Your word is as good as Your bond. Thank You for inviting me to enter into a covenant with You. I earnestly desire to be assured that You are committed to me forever. I long to belong to You. So right now, I confess to You that I am a sinner and have no merit of my own to deserve or earn this privilege. Instead, I have a strong tendency to do the wrong thing. To sin. So I confess to you my _____ [fill in the blank with specific sins that come to your mind].

I'm willing to turn away from my sin, to stop sinning, but I need Your help. I believe Jesus died on the Cross for me. Right now, I choose to "drink the cup" of His blood shed on the Cross, applying His death to make atonement for my sin.

Please forgive me and cleanse me of all my sin and guilt. And I choose to "eat the bread" of His body, surrendering every part of my life to His authority. Please come into my heart and be Lord of my life.

I believe Jesus rose up from the dead to give me eternal life. I understand that eternal life means that Heaven is now my home, but I also understand that it includes the believer's birthright that floods me with blessing after blessing. Without doubt, the most precious blessing of all is entering into this covenant and a personal love relationship with You. Thank You for hearing this prayer. I take You at Your word. I climb into the wheelbarrow and trust myself to You completely. Forever.

For the glory of Your great name, Amen.[1]

CHAPTER 20

Commitment MAKES A DIFFERENCE

If serving the LORD seems undesirable
to you, then choose for yourselves
this day whom you will serve. . . . But
as for me and my household, we will
serve the LORD.

JOSHUA 24:15

The Bible doesn't tell us when Daniel first chose to commit his life to God. But it is obvious he had made that choice by the time we meet him in the first chapter of Daniel. At great risk to himself and his three friends, he made his faith in God his priority when he refused to defile himself with the king's food. We know from Scripture that to refuse the king *anything* could have a grave outcome. We read of the king casting men into a fiery furnace (3:15–23), of condemning men to be cut into pieces while they were still alive (2:5). Daniel knew the risks. And yet, he took the chance, choosing to obey God rather than man. The result of that one choice rippled out with broad consequences until he became one of the greatest men of his day, as well as in biblical history. Not only was he a powerful leader under four emperors covering two world empires, but his prayer for his own Jewish people resulted in their release after seventy years of captivity in Babylon.

The apostle Paul made the choice to commit his life to Jesus Christ, then testified, "Here is a trustworthy saying that deserves full acceptance: Christ Jesus

came into the world to save sinners—of whom I am the worst. But for that very reason I was shown mercy so that in me, the worst of sinners, Christ Jesus might display his unlimited patience as an example for those who would believe on him and receive eternal life" (1 Timothy 1:15–16). Paul went on to turn the entire world of his day upside down as he proclaimed the Gospel through his testimony, through his preaching, as well as through his writing which comprises most of the New Testament (see Acts 17:1–6). Within approximately two hundred years after Paul's life, the Gospel had so permeated the known world that Christianity was adopted as the official religion of the Roman Empire. That revolution began with a choice.

William Carey (1761–1834), a cobbler who heard God's call in the quietness of his shoe shop, made the choice to commit his life to Jesus. He testified, "If it be the duty of all men to believe the Gospel . . . then it be the duty of those who are entrusted

> No one is an island to himself because our choices make a difference for generations to come.

with the Gospel to endeavor to make it known among all nations." It is said that he then burst into tears and

responded with the words of Isaiah, "Here am I; send me" (Isaiah 6:8 KJV). Carey proclaimed the Gospel in India for forty-one years. He is considered the greatest missionary of the modern world. He translated and published the Scriptures into forty different languages and successfully worked to ban *sati*, the practice of burning widows alive when their husbands died. One of his sermon titles that has been quoted thousands of times seems to summarize his life of service: "Expect great things from God. Attempt great things for God." His commitment began with a choice.

As a young man, Hudson Taylor (1832–1905) forsook the faith of his parents, but at the age of seventeen, he made the choice to embrace Jesus as his personal Lord and Savior. As a British missionary, he founded the China Inland Mission in order to proclaim the Gospel for fifty-one years in every province of China. As a result of his one choice, China was changed and today the Chinese church is one of the largest, fastest-growing churches in the world.

One man, named Azzam, a former pirate somewhere in Somalia today, rides in coffins, under corpses, because he knows Somali Muslims will not open a casket or touch a dead body, much less look

under it. This is how Azzam "safely" travels outside of Somalia, where he then is given a load of Bibles in Kenya. He travels back into Somalia in a coffin, under a corpse, with the precious cargo of God's Word, which many people in his area are desperate to read. How could he have ever come to the decision to engage in such a mission?

Azzam had been born and raised a Muslim but had been having dreams of Jesus. He had sought out his imam for answers, but the man had violently berated and beaten him. When his mother discovered he was having Jesus dreams, she commanded him to leave the home for his own protection and never come back. He did.

He walked for miles and miles, quite sure his father would be unable to find him. But he was wrong. His father was a powerful warlord who located him quickly and sent Azzam a package. When Azzam opened it, he was shocked and sickened to find his mother, cut up into small pieces. A photograph had been included inside the plastic bag. It was a picture of his mother kneeling in front of two men who had their knives raised over her.

The day Azzam opened that "package" is the day he made the choice to commit his life to Jesus Christ as his Lord and Savior.

This is where the story gets even more incredible, because Azzam sought out the two men who had butchered his mother. He told them that he forgave them. He also told them that Jesus loved them and that He could forgive murderers. The two men, Mahdi and Yasin, embraced the Gospel and chose to commit their lives to Jesus too. Then they confided to Azzam, "As we killed your mother, her last words were, 'Jesus, Jesus, I love You.'" And while Somalia has yet to be changed, it will be. One choice at a time.[1]

Daniel made the choice to commit his life to the glory of God. And he kept that commitment until his death.

THINK ABOUT IT

God is the God of second chances. Don't miss the opportunity to make the best choice of your life: turn to God, confess your wrong choices, ask Him to redeem them . . . then make the next right choice and commit your life to living for Him as your Savior and Lord. Only eternity will reveal the impact your choice will make on the generations that follow.

Lord God of Eternity,

We worship you as the Great I AM, the One who never changes. You are the same yesterday, as You are today, as You will be tomorrow and forevermore.

We praise You as One who committed Yourself to us—even to death on the Cross. You then, in turn, call us to deny ourselves, our wants, our goals, our will, and take up the cross of Your will every day, and come follow You.

We are fully aware that if we choose to follow You, You will lead us to a cross. But help us never to forget that after the Cross comes the resurrection and the power and the glory and the crown!

As I recommit myself to following You, mold and make me into a disciple who so clearly reflects You in all I say and do, that succeeding generations will be irresistibly drawn to commit their lives to follow You, too.

For the glory of Your great name, Amen.

Date: _____

NOTES

Chapter 2: Worship Makes a Difference

1. Hebrews 1:1–3.
2. Psalm 2.
3. Psalm 46.

Chapter 3: Loyalty Makes a Difference

1. Matthew 10:32.

Chapter 4: Prayer Partners Make a Difference

1. 1 Timothy 2:5.
2. Hebrews 7:25.
3. James 5:16.

Chapter 5: Praying for Others Makes a Difference

1. As the honorary chair for the National Day of Prayer 2014, I was asked to write the prayer that was used across the nation.

Chapter 6: Praying God's Word Makes a Difference

1. Ezekiel 36:37.

Chapter 7: Attitude Makes a Difference

1. Romans 8:28.
2. Joseph Lenard, "Jesus' Birth—the Wise Men (Magi)," Truth in Scripture, (January 3, 2017), https:// truthinscripture.net/2017/01/03/ jesus-birth-the-wise-men-magi/.

Chapter 8: Listening Makes a Difference

1. *Daily Light* (Nashville: J. Countryman, 1998). The foreword of this daily devotional will explain what a meaningful tool this has been in my family as the Truth has been passed down from generation to generation.
2. My mother taught me as a girl to put my name in the verses I read to make them more personally mine. I still do this today.
3. Haggai 2:4; Ephesians 6:10; Zechariah 8:9; Judges 6:14; 2 Corinthians 4:1; Galatians 6:9 all from the NKJV.
4. Visit my website: www. annegrahamlotz.org, click on *Studies in God's Word*, and then click on *Journey to Jesus*. It's a free resource that will lead you through the steps of how to listen to God's voice.
5. Isaiah 51:16.
6. Genesis 1:3; John 1:1–3.
7. Isaiah 55:9.
8. 1 John 1:5.
9. Deuteronomy 32:47.

10. Psalm 119:89.

11. James 1:17.

Chapter 9: A Daily Prayer Time Makes a Difference

1. Daniel 6:10.

Chapter 10: Perseverance Makes a Difference

1. A few of the many biblical reasons for unanswered prayer are: unconfessed sin (Isaiah 59:2), arrogance (Job 35:12–13), and wrong motives (James 4:3).

2. See Colossians 2:15, Revelation 5:5, 11–13.

3. Ephesians 6:13.

Chapter 11: Desperate Prayers Make a Difference

1. The story of Dori can be found in Tom Doyle, *Killing Christians* (Nashville: W Publishing Group, 2015), 43–73.

2. Luke 5:32.

3. Revelation 3:17.

4. Ibid.

5. John 16:24.

Chapter 15: Confession Makes a Difference

1. Charles G. Finney, *How to Experience Revival*, (New Kensington, PA: Whitaker House, 1984).

2. Isaiah 61:10.

3. From Arthur Bennett, *The Valley of Vision: A Collection of Puritan Prayers and Devotions* (Edinburgh, The Banner of Truth Trust, 1975), 76, 6.

Chapter 17: Forgiveness Makes a Difference

1. The story is true, but the name has been changed.

2. This story is adapted from Anne Graham Lotz, *Wounded by God's People* (Grand Rapids, MI: Zondervan, 2013), 198–203.

3. The opening paragraphs of this prayer are taken from *The Valley of Vision* (Edinburgh: The Banner of Truth Trust, 1975), "The Precious Blood," 41.

Chapter 18: Humility Makes a Difference

1. The parable is found in Luke 18:9–14.

Chapter 19: A Personal Relationship with God Makes a Difference

1. This prayer is based on the following verses: Matthew 24:35; Romans 3:23; 1 John 1:8–10; Acts 3:19; Ephesians 1:7–8; John 6:49–51; 1 Corinthians 11:23–26; John 3:14–18, 1:16.

Chapter 20: Commitment Makes a Difference

1. Tom Doyle, *Killing Christians* (Nashville: W Publishing Group, 2015), 1–17.